KALI LINUX

SERIES

The complete Basic guide in Kali linux for Hackers Getting Started with Networking and Scripting

Robert White

© **Copyright 2021 by - All rights reserved.**

This document is geared towards providing exact and reliable information in regards to the topic and issue covered. The publication is sold with the idea that the publisher is not required to render accounting, officially permitted, or otherwise, qualified services. If advice is necessary, legal or professional, a practiced individual in the profession should be ordered.

- From a Declaration of Principles which was accepted and approved equally by a Committee of the American Bar Association and a Committee of Publishers and Associations.

In no way is it legal to reproduce, duplicate, or transmit any part of this document in either electronic means or in printed format. Recording of this publication is strictly prohibited and any storage of this document is not allowed unless with written permission from the publisher. All rights reserved.

The information provided herein is stated to be truthful and consistent, in that any liability, in terms of inattention or otherwise, by any usage or abuse of any policies, processes, or directions contained within is the solitary and utter responsibility of the recipient reader. Under no circumstances will any legal responsibility or blame be held against the publisher for any reparation, damages, or monetary loss due to the information herein, either directly or indirectly.

Respective authors own all copyrights not held by the publisher.

The information herein is offered for informational purposes solely and is universal as such. The presentation of the information is without a contract or any type of guarantee assurance.

The trademarks that are used are without any consent, and the publication of the trademark is without permission or backing by the trademark owner. All trademarks and brands within this book are for clarifying purposes only and are owned by the owners themselves, not affiliated with this document.

KALI LINUX

INTRODUCTION	**14**
CHAPTER 1	**17**
1.1 KALI RELATIONSHIP WITH DEBIAN	17
1.1.1 Package Flow	*17*
1.1.2. Management of Difference with Debian	*18*
1.2 USE CASES AND PURPOSE	19
CHAPTER 2	**24**
2.1 KALI LINUX MAIN FEATURES	24
2.1.1 Live System	*24*
2.1.2 Completely Customizable	*25*
2.1.3 Custom Linux Kernel	*25*
2.1.4 Usable on a Huge Range of ARM Systems	*26*
2.1.5 A Trustable Operating System	*26*
2.1.6 Forensic Mode	*26*
2.2 POLICIES	27
2.2.1 Network Services Disabled via Default	*27*
2.2.2 Curated series of packages	*27*
CHAPTER 3	**29**
3.1 FUNDAMENTALS OF LINUX	29
3.2 DRIVING HARDWARE	29
3.3 UNIFYING REPORT SYSTEMS	30
3.4 MANAGING PROGRESS	33
3.5 RIGHTS MANAGEMENT	34
CHAPTER 4	**35**
4.1 INSTALLATION	35
4.2 REQUIREMENTS FOR INSTALLATION	35
4.3 INSTALLATION ON A HARD DRIVE	35
4.4. PLAIN INSTALLATION	36
4.4.1 Booting and starting the Installer	*36*
4.4.2 Selecting the Language	*37*
4.4.3 Selecting the Country	*38*
4.4.4 Selecting the Keyboard format	*39*

4.4.5 Detecting hardware 40
4.4.6 Loading Components 40
4.4.7 Detecting network hardware 41
4.4.8 Configuring the Network 41
4.4.9 user Creation 42
4.4.10 Configuring the Clock 43
4.5 DETECTING DISKS AND OTHER SYSTEMS 44

CHAPTER 5 49

5.1 CONFIGURATION OF KALI LINUX 49
5.2 CONFIGURING THE NETWORK 49
    5.2.1 On Command Line with Ifupdown 50
5.3 MANAGING UNIX USERS AND UNIX CORPORATIONS 52
    5.3.1 Creating User Accounts 52
    5.3.2 Modifying an existing Account or Password 53
    5.3.3 Disabling an Account 54
    5.3.4 Management of Unix Groups 54
5.4 CONFIGURATION OF SPECIFIC PROGRAM 54
    5.4.1 Configuring a Specific Software Program 55
    5.4.2 Configuring SSH Remote Logins 56
    5.4.3 Configuring postgresql Databases 56
5.5 TYPE OF CONNECTION AND CLIENT AUTHENTICATION 56
5.6 CREATING USERS AND DATABASES 57
5.7 MANAGING POSTGRESQL CLUSTERS 57
5.8 CONFIGURING APACHE 58
5.9 SERVICE MANAGEMENT 59

CHAPTER 6 60

6.1 KALI LINUX: SECURING AND MONITORING 60
6.2 SECURITY POLICY 60
6.3 POSSIBLE SECURITY MEASURES 62
    6.3.1 On a Server 63
    6.3.2 On a laptop 63
6.4 SECURING NETWORK OFFERINGS 64
6.5 FIREWALL OR PACKET FILTERING 64
    6.5.1 Netfilter behavior 65
    6.5.2 Syntax of iptables and ip6tables 69
    6.5.3 Creating Rules 70
    6.5.4 Installing in the rules at every Boot 72

- 6.6 LOGGING AND MONITORING.. 72
  - *6.6.1 monitoring Logs with logcheck* 73
  - *6.6.2 Monitoring Interest in Real Time* 73
- **CONCLUSION** **75**

LINUX

INTRODUCTION	79
CHAPTER 1	**81**
1.1 FEDORA LINUX	81
1.2 COMMAND	81
1.3 USERS & SUPERUSERS	84
CHAPTER 2	**85**
2.1 INPUT AND OUTPUT	85
2.2 STANDARD HEADING	87
2.2.1 ls [options] [files]	*87*
2.2.2 Stdin	*87*
2.2.3 Stdout	*87*
2.2.4 File	*87*
2.2.5 .Opt	*89*
2.2.6 Help	*89*
2.2.7 Standard symbols	*89*
2.2.8 The echo command, your friend	*90*
2.3 GETTING THE HELP	90
2.3.1 Run the man command	*90*
2.3.2 Run the info command	*91*
2.3.3 Use the help option (if any)	*91*
2.3.4 Examine the directory /usr/share/doc	*91*
2.4 GNOME AND KDE HELP	92
2.4.1 Usenet newsgroups	*92*
2.4.2 Google	*92*
2.4.3 Fedora: a primary View	*92*
CHAPTER 3	**96**
3.1 ROLE OF THE SHELL	96
3.1.1 How to run a shell	*96*
CHAPTER 4	**98**
4.1 SHUTDOWNS, LOGINS AND LOGOUTS	98
4.2 SHUTDOWNS	98

9

CHAPTER 5 101

- 5.1 Filesystem 101
- 5.2 Home Directories 103
- 5.3 HOME Directories 104
- 5.4 System Directories 104
- 5.5 Categories for programs 105
- 5.6 Categories for documentation 106
- 5.7 Categories for configuration 106
- 5.8 Classes for programming 106
- 5.9 Categories for web files 106
- 5.10 Categories for display 107
- 5.11 Categories for hardware 107
- 5.12 Categories for runtime files 107
- 5.13 Path of directories section 2: scope 108
- 5.14 Path of directories section 3: scope 109
- 5.15 Directories of Operating System 109
- 5.16 Protection of File 111

CHAPTER 6 112

- 6.1 The Shell 112
- 6.2 Program vs shells 113
- 6.3 Features of Bash 113
- 6.4 Wildcards 114
- 6.5 Brace expansion 114
- 6.6 Tilde expansion 115
- 6.7 Shell variables 115
- 6.8 Search path 117
- 6.9 Aliases 118
- 6.10 Input/output redirection 118
- 6.11 Pipes 119
- 6.12 Combining commands 120
- 6.13 Quoting 120
- 6.14 Escaping 121
- 6.15 Command line editing 123

CHAPTER 7 124

- 7.1 Killing command line 124
- 7.2 Terminating a Shell 125

7.3 TAILORING SHELLS' BEHAVIOR 125
7.4 INSTALLING PROGRAM 125
    7.4.1 *.tar.gz files, *.tar.Z documents, and *.tar.bz2 files..........................125
    7.4.2 *.rpm files...126
7.5 UP2DATE 127
7.6 RPM..128
7.7 LS..128
7.8 CP 129
7.9 LN 129
7.10 DIRECTORY OPERATIONS 130

CHAPTER 8...134

8.1 FILE CREATION AND EDITING 134
8.2 EMACS...137
8.3 VIM 137
8.4 UMASK...137
8.5 SOFFICE 139
8.6 ABIWORD 139
    8.7 gnumeric..139
8.8 FILE PROPERTIES 140
8.9 FIND LOCATION 149
8.10 INDEXING OPTIONS 150
8.11 FILE TEXT MANIPULATION 152
8.12 FILE COMPARISON 153

CHAPTER 9...156

9.1 DISKS AND FILE SYSTEM..156
9.2 PARTITIONING AND FORMATTING DISKS 161
9.3 BACKUPS AND REMOTE STORAGE 161
9.4 FILE PRINTING 162
9.5 SPELLING OPERATIONS 163
9.6 VIEWING PROCESSES 165
9.7 CONTROLLING METHODS 165
9.8 CUSTOMERS AND THEIR ENVIRONMENT 169

CHAPTER 10...172

10.1 NETWORK CONNECTIONS 172
10.2 EVOLUTION 178
10.3 MUTT [OPTIONS] 179

10.4 MAIL 180
13.1 CONCLUSION 183
   13.1.1 Final words 183

Introduction

Kali Linux is the world's most effective and famous penetration testing platform, used by safety specialists in an extensive range of specializations, which include penetration testing out, forensics, reverse engineering, and vulnerability assessment. It is the fruit of years of refinement and the end result of a continuous evolution of the platform, from Whoppix to WHAX, to go into reverse, and now to an entire penetration testing framework leveraging many capabilities of Debian GNU/Linux and the vibrant open supply network global. Kali Linux has no longer been constructed to be a simple collection of gear, but alternatively a flexible framework that expert penetration testers, security fanatics, college students, and amateurs can personalize to fit their precise needs. Kali Linux is not merely a set of numerous statistics protection tools which might be established on a trendy Debian base and preconfigured to get you up and walking proper away. To get the maximum out of Kali, it is critical to have a radical knowledge of its powerful Debian GNU/Linux underpinnings and getting to know how you could position them to use on your surroundings. Although Kali is decidedly multiple reasons, it is in most cases designed to useful resource in penetration testing out. The goal of this book is not always simplest that will help you experience at home when you use Kali Linux, but also to assist enhance your expertise and streamline your revel in in order that whilst you are engaged in a penetration check and time is of the essence, you won't want to fear about dropping valuable minutes to install new software or permit a new network provider. On this book, we are able to introduce you first to Linux, then we are able to dive deeper as we introduce you to the nuances unique to Kali Linux, so you recognize precisely what goes on beneath the hood. That is priceless knowhow to have, in particular whilst you are attempting to work below tight time constraints. It isn't always uncommon to require this intensity of expertise while you are getting set up, troubleshooting a trouble, struggling to bend a system in your will, parsing output from a tool, or leveraging Kali in a larger scale surroundings.

The Kali Linux project started out quietly in 2012, whilst Offensive protection determined that they wanted to update their venerable back off Linux undertaking, which turned into manually maintained, with something that would end up a true Debian derivative, complete with all the required infrastructure and improved packaging techniques. The choice changed into made to construct Kali on pinnacle of the Debian distribution due to the fact it is far widely recognized for its quality, balance, and huge selection of to be had software. The primary release (model 1.0) came about twelve months later, in March 2013, and become primarily based on Debian 7 "Wheezy", Debian's solid distribution at the time. In that first 12 months of development, they packaged hundreds of penetration testing related applications and constructed the infrastructure. Even though the number of packages is vast, the application listing has been meticulously curated, dropping programs that not worked or that duplicated functions already to be had in better programs.

Throughout the 2 years following model 1.0, Kali launched many incremental updates, increasing the variety of to be had packages and enhancing hardware aid, thanks to more recent kernel related. With some investment in continuous integration, it was ensured that everyone important programs had been kept in an installable nation and that customized live pictures (an indicator of the distribution) could usually be created. In 2015, while Debian 8 "Jessie" came out, the work to rebase Kali Linux on top. While Kali Linux 1.x averted the GNOME Shell (counting on GNOME Fallback as an alternative), on this version it was decided to include and decorate it: the few GNOME Shell extensions to collect lacking capabilities, maximum appreciably the packages menu. The result of that work became Kali Linux 2.0, posted in August 2015. In parallel, it elevated the efforts to make certain that Kali Linux always has the new version of all penetration testing out packages. Unfortunately, that aim changed into a chunk at odds with the usage of Debian Stable as a base for the distribution, as it required us to backport many packages. That is because of the reality that Debian solid puts a priority on the steadiness of the software program, often causing an extended put off from the discharge of an upstream update to while it is far included into the distribution. Given our investment in continuous integration, it became quite a natural pass to rebase Kali Linux on top of Debian Testing so that it was ought to benefit from the cutting-edge version of all Debian packages as quickly as they have been to be had. Debian testing has a miles more aggressive update cycle, which is greater compatible with the philosophy of Kali Linux. This is, in essence, the idea of Kali Rolling. Whilst the rolling distribution has been to be had for quite some time, Kali 2016.1 changed into the primary launch to officially embrace the rolling nature of that distribution: when you set up the day Kali release, your system without a doubt tracks the Kali Rolling distribution and every unmarried day you get new updates. Inside the past, Kali releases were snapshots of the underlying Debian distribution with Kaliprecise packages injected into it. A rolling distribution has many advantages, but it additionally comes with multiple demanding situations, both for those folks who are constructing the distribution and for the users who have to cope with a continuous float of updates and every so often backwards incompatible modifications. This book pursuits to present you the understanding required to deal with everything you could come upon while coping with your Kali Linux set up.

Chapter 1

1.1 Kali Relationship with Debian

The Kali Linux distribution is primarily based on Debian Testing. Consequently, most of the packages to be had in Kali Linux come directly from this Debian repository. At the same time as Kali Linux relies heavily on Debian, it's also absolutely independent within the experience that we've got our personal infrastructure and preserve the liberty to make any adjustments we need.

1.1.1 Package Flow

At the Debian side, the individuals are operating each day on updating applications and importing them to the Debian risky distribution (unstable is also called sid). From there, programs migrate to the Debian testing out distribution once the most difficult bugs had been taken out. The migration process additionally guarantees that no dependencies are broken in Debian testing out. The purpose is that testing is continually in a usable (or maybe releasable!) State. Debian testing goals align quite properly with the ones of Kali Linux, so we picked it because the base. To add the Kali particular applications within the distribution, we observe a twostep procedure.

First, we take Debian testing out and fore inject our own Kali applications (located in our kali dev repository) to construct the kali dev repository. This repository will break now and again: for instance, our Kali unique packages may not be installable until they had been recompiled against more recent libraries. In different situations, applications that we've forked may additionally be up to date, both to come to be installable once more, or to restoration the install ability of another bundle that relies upon on a more modern version of the forked package deal. Anyhow, kali dev is not for end users. Kali rolling is the distribution that Kali Linux users are predicted to track and is constructed out of kali dev within the identical manner that Debian testing out is built out of Debian volatile. Packages migrate simplest while all dependencies may be glad within the target distribution.

1.1.2. Management of Difference with Debian

As a layout selection, we attempt to minimize the wide variety of forked packages as a lot as feasible. However, in an effort to put into effect some of Kali's unique functions, a few modifications need to be made. To limit the impact of these changes, we strive to ship them upstream, both via integrating the function directly, or through including the desired hooks so that it is straightforward to enable the

18

desired features without further editing the upstream programs themselves.

The Kali package Tracker enables us to keep track of our divergence with Debian. At any time, we will look up which package has been forked and whether it's miles in sync with Debian, or if an update is needed. All our programs are maintained in Git repositories web hosting a Debian branch and a Kali department aspect with the aid of aspect. Thanks to this, updating a forked package deal is an easy step technique: replace the Debian branch after which merge it into the Kali department. While the range of forked packages in Kali is distinctly low, the range of additional packages is as an alternative excessive: in January 2021 there were almost 500. Maximum of these packages are free software complying with the Debian unfastened software program Guidelines and our final aim would be to maintain the ones packages within Debian on every occasion possible. This is why we attempt to comply with the Debian Policy and to follow the coolest packaging practices utilized in Debian. Sadly, there also are pretty a few exceptions in which right packaging turned into nearly not possible to create. Because of time being scarce, few packages had been pushed to Debian.

1.2 Use Cases and Purpose

While Kali's awareness may be fast summarized as "penetration testing and protection auditing", there are numerous special tasks worried behind the ones activities. Kali Linux is built as a platform, as it includes many tools masking very distinct use cases (although they may absolutely be used in mixture for the duration of a penetration take a look at).

As an instance, Kali Linux may be used on various styles of computers: obviously on the desktops of penetration testers, however additionally on servers of system directors wishing to display their net paintings, on the workstations of forensic analysts, and more , on stealthy embedded de vices, generally with ARM cpus, that may be dropped within the range of a wireless community or plugged inside the desktop of target customers. Many ARM systems are also ideal attack systems because of their small form elements and occasional power necessities. Kali Linux also can be deployed in the cloud to fast construct a farm of password cracking systems and on mobile phones and pills to permit for truly transportable penetration trying out. But that is not all; penetration testers also need servers: to use collaboration software inside a campaigns, to run vulnerability scanning equipment, and different associated activities.

As soon as you've got booted Kali, you will fast discover that Kali Linux's important menu is organized by theme across the various styles of obligations and activities which can be applicable for penetration testers and different information protection specialists as shown in Figure.

Figure 1.1

These tasks and activities consists of:

- **Information Gathering:** Collecting data about the target network and its structure, discovering computer systems, their running systems, and the services that they run. Identifying potentially sensitive elements of the information system. Extracting all styles of listings from jogging directory services.
- **Vulnerability evaluation:** speedy testing out whether a local or remote system is tormented by some of known vulnerabilities or insecure configurations. Vulnerability scanners use databases containing heaps of signatures to discover capacity vulnerabilities.
- **Internet utility analysis:** figuring out misconfigurations and safety weaknesses in internet applications. It's miles important to identify and mitigate these problems for the reason that the general public avail potential of those programs makes them ideal goals for attackers.
- **Database evaluation:** From square injection to attacking credentials, database attacks are a not unusual vector for attackers. Tools that check for attack vectors starting from sq. Injection to data extraction and evaluation can be discovered here.
- **Password attacks:** Authentication structures are usually a pass to assault vector. Many beneficial tools may be located here, from online password attack equipment to offline attacks in opposition to the encryption or hashing systems.
- **Wireless attacks:** The pervasive nature of WIFI networks way that they may constantly be a generally attacked vector. With its extensive variety of aid for multiple wireless playing cards, Kali is an obvious choice for assaults against more than one sorts of WIFI networks.
- **Reverse Engineering:** reverse engineering is an interest with many functions. In help of offensive activities, it's miles one of the primary methods for vulnerability identification and make

the most improvement. On the protecting side, it is used to research malware employed in targeted assaults. On this capacity, the aim is to pick out the competencies of a given piece of tradecraft.

- **Exploitation tool:** Exploiting or taking benefit of a (previously diagnosed) vulnerability, lets in you to advantage manage of a remote system (or tool). This access can then be used for further privilege escalation assaults, both regionally locally at the compromised system, or on different systems on hand on its nearby network. This category includes a number of gear and utilities that simplify the manner of writing your own exploits.
- **Sniffing & Spoofing:** Gaining access to the data as they travel across the network is often advantageous for an attacker. Right here you can discover spoofing tools that will let you impersonate a valid person as well as sniffing tools that will let you seize and examine statistics proper off the twine. Whilst used together, these gear can be very effective.
- **Post Exploitation:** Once you have gained access to a system, you will often want to maintain that degree of get right of entry to or expand manipulate by using laterally transferring across the community. Equipment that help in those dreams are found right here.
- **Forensics:** Forensic Linux live boot environments had been very famous for years now. Kali incorporates a huge range of famous Linux based totally forensic tools permitting you to do everything from preliminary triage, to information imaging, to complete evaluation and case control.
- **Reporting equipment:** A penetration check is handiest whole once the findings have been stated. This category carries equipment to assist collate the information amassed from data

collecting tools, find out nonobvious relationships, and produce the entirety together in diverse reviews.
- **Social Engineering tools:** whilst the technical aspect is properly secured, there may be regularly the possibility of exploiting human conduct as an attack vector. Given the proper impact, people can frequently be caused to take moves that compromise the security of the surroundings. Did the USB key that the secretary just plugged in contain an innocent PDF? Or become it additionally a malicious program that established a backdoor? Turned into the banking internet site the accountant just logged into the predicted website or a great replica used for phishing functions? This category contains tools that resource in these forms of attacks.

Chapter 2

2.1 Kali Linux Main Features

Kali Linux is a Linux distribution that contains its personal collection of loads of software program tool specifically tailor made for their target customers penetration testers and other protection professionals. It also comes with an installation software to completely setup Kali Linux as the main operating system on any pc. That is quite similar to all other existing Linux distributions but there are different features that differentiate Kali Linux, lots of that are tailored to the precise needs of penetration testers.

2.1.1 Live System

Alongside the main installer ISO images, Kali Linux offers a separate live ISO picture to download. This lets you to use Kali Linux as a bootable live system. In different words, you can use Kali Linux without installing it, just by booting the ISO picture (normally after having copied the photo onto a USB key). The live system carries the tool most usually utilized by penetration testers, so even in case your daily system is not Kali Linux, you may definitely insert the disk or USB key and reboot to run Kali. But remember that the default configuration will now not keep adjustments among reboots. If you configure endurance with a USB key, then you may tweak the gadget on your liking (adjust config files, store reports, improve software program, and installation extra programs, as an example), and the changes could be retained across reboots.

2.1.2 Completely Customizable

Kali Linux is constructed by way of penetration testers for penetration testers; however, we take into account that not everyone will trust our design choices or preference of equipment to include by using default. With this in thoughts, we constantly make certain that Kali Linux is easy to personalize based on your personal wishes and likeness. To this end, we publish the live build configuration used to build the legit Kali images so that you can customize it for your liking. It is very clean to start from this published configuration and put in force numerous modifications primarily based in your desires way to the flexibility of live build.

Stay construct consists of many features to regulate the installed system, installation supplementary files, install additional applications, run arbitrary instructions, and trade the values presided to deb conf.

2.1.3 Custom Linux Kernel

Kali Linux continually gives a customized current Linux kernel, based at the model in Debian unstable. This ensures solid hardware aid, in particular for a huge range of WIFI systems. The kernel is patched for WIFI injection assist because many WIFI security evaluation gear depend upon this selection. For the reason that many hardware system require up to date firmware files (observed in /lib/firmware/), Kali installs all of them by default which include the firmware available in Debian's not free section. The ones aren't set up with the aid of default in Debian, because they are closed supply and hence not part of Debian proper.

2.1.4 Usable on a Huge Range of ARM Systems

Kali Linux gives binary applications for the armel, armhf, and arm64 ARM architectures. Way to the effortlessly installable pictures provided by using Offensive security, Kali Linux can be deployed on many exciting systems, from smartphones and drugs to wireless routers and computers of numerous styles and sizes.

2.1.5 A Trustable Operating System

Users of a safety distribution rightfully need to recognize that it could be depended on and that it has been evolved in undeniable sight, allowing all people to look at the supply code. Kali Linux is evolved via a small team of knowledgeable developers running transparently and following the excellent protection practices: they add signed supply packages, which might be then built on devoted construct daemons. The applications are then check summed and disbursed as part of a signed repository. The work done out at the applications can be completely reviewed through the packaging Git repositories (which incorporate signed tags) which might be used to build the Kali source programs. The evolution of every package deal also can be observed thru the Kali package tracker.

2.1.6 Forensic Mode

In general, whilst doing forensic paintings on a system, you need to avoid any hobby that would modify the information on the analyzed gadget in any way. Alas, current computing system environments have a tendency to interfere with this objective by means of trying to automount any disk(s) they detect. To avoid this conduct, Kali Linux has a forensics mode that can be enabled from the boot menu: it's going to disable all such features. The live system is specifically beneficial for forensics functions, due to the fact it is feasible to reboot any desktop into a Kali Linux system without getting access to or enhancing its hard disks.

2.2 Policies

At the same time as Kali Linux strives to follow the Debian policy whenever feasible, there are some areas in which we made significantly exceptional layout choices because of the unique needs of protection professionals.

2.2.1 Network Services Disabled via Default

In contrast to Debian, Kali Linux disables any established provider that could concentrate on a public internet work interface by using default, such as HTTP and SSH. The intent at the back of this selection is to reduce exposure at some stage in a penetration check whilst it's far unfavorable to announce your presence and risk detection due to unexpected network interactions. You can still manually allow any offerings of your selecting by way of going for walks sudo systemctl permit carrier.

2.2.2 Curated series of packages

Debian ambitions to be the normal running gadget and places very few limits on what receives packaged, supplied that each bundle has a maintainer. By way of comparison, Kali Linux does not package every penetration trying out tool available. As an alternative, we purpose to offer most effective the best freely licensed tools masking maximum obligations that a penetration tester may want to perform. Kali builders working as penetration testers force the selection procedure and we leverage their experience and expertise to make enlightened selections. In a few instances this is a depend on reality, but there are other, more difficult alternatives that honestly come right down to private choice.

Right here are some of the factors considered while a new application receives evaluated:

- The adequate usefulness of the application in context of penetration testing
- The distinctive unique functionality of the features of application.
- The license of the application
- The resource application requirements

Retaining an up to date and beneficial penetration checking out system repository is a challenging mission. We welcome system recommendations inside a dedicated class (new tool requests) in the Kali bug Tracker. New tool requests are first class received when the submission is properly offered, which includes an explanation of why the tool is useful, the way it compares to different similar programs, and so on.

Chapter 3

3.1 Fundamentals of Linux

The term "Linux" is often used to refer the entire running system, however in reality, Linux is the operating system kernel, that's commenced by way of the boot loader, that's itself commenced through the BIOS/UEFI. The kernel assumes a position much like that of a conductor in an orchestra it ensures coordination among hardware and software program. This role consists of coping with hardware, processes, customers, permissions, and the report gadget. The kernel gives a commonplace base to all other programs on the system and commonly runs in ring 0, also known as kernel space.
The User Space We use the term user space to lump collectively everything that happens outside of the kernel. Some of the programs running in user space are many core utilities from the GNU project, maximum of which might be meant to be run from the command line.

3.2 Driving hardware

The kernel is tasked, first and primary, with controlling the desktop's hardware additives. It detects and configures them when the pc powers on, or when a system is inserted or removed (as an example, a USB system). It additionally makes them to be had to higher stage software program, via a simplified programming interface, so programs can take benefit of gadgets without having to address information along with which extension slot a choice board is plugged into. The programming interface also presents an abstraction layer;

this allows video conferencing software program, for example, to apply a webcam irrespective of its maker and version. The software program can use the Video for Linux (V4L) interface and the kernel will translate function calls of the interface into actual hardware commands wished by way of the unique webcam in use. The kernel exports facts about detected hardware via the /proc/ and /sys/ virtual record systems. Programs frequently get admission to gadgets by way of way of files created within /dev/. Precise files represent disk drives (for instance, /dev/sda), walls (/dev/sda1), mice (/dev/enter/mouse0), keyboards (/dev/input/event0), sound cards (/dev/snd/*), serial ports (/dev/ttys*), and different components.

There are two forms of system files: block and character. The former has traits of a block of information: It has a finite size, and you could get right of entry to bytes at any function inside the block. The latter behaves like a drift of characters. You can study and write characters, but you cannot seek to given role/position and trade arbitrary bytes. To find out the form of a given tool report, check out the first letter inside the output of ls -l. It's far either b, for block systems, or c, for character systems:

```
$       ls      -l      /dev/sda                                /dev/ttys0
brw-rw---- 1 root disk 8,    0   May 24 07:44 /dev/sda
Crw-rw---- 1 root dialout 4, 64 May 30 06:59 /dev/ttys0
```

As you may expect, disk drives and partitions use block systems, while mouse, keyboard, and serial ports use individual gadgets. In each instances, the programming interface consists of system specific commands that can be invoked through the ioctl system name.

3.3 Unifying report systems

File systems are an outstanding factor of the kernel. Unix like systems merge all the record stores into a single hierarchy, which lets in users and packages to access statistics via knowing its place within that hierarchy. The starting point of this hierarchical tree is known as the basis, represented via the "/" person. This listing can contain named subdirectories. As an example, the home subdirectory of / is called /home/. This subdirectory can, in turn, contain other subdirectories, and so forth. Every listing also can contain files, wherein the information could be saved. Thus, /domestic/kali/desktop/hiya.txt refers to a report named hiya.txt stored in the desktop subdirectory of the kali subdirectory of the house directory, gift in the root. The kernel interprets between this naming system and the storage location on a disk. Not like different systems, Linux possesses simplest one such hierarchy, and it may integrate information from several disks. This sort of disks becomes the foundation, and the others are hooked up on directories in the hierarchy (the Linux command is called mount). Those different disks are then available under the mount points. This permits storing users' domestic directories (historically stored within /domestic/) on a separate tough disk, for you to include the kali listing (together with domestic directories of other customers). Once you mount the disk on /domestic/, these directories become available at their regular locations, and paths along with /domestic/kali/desktop/hey.txt keep working.

There are many file system formats, corresponding to many ways of bodily storing records on disks. The most widely known are ext2, ext3, and ext4, but others exist. For example, VFAT is the filesystem that was historically used by DOS and Microsoft windows operating structures. Linux's support for VFAT permits tough disks to be reachable underneath Kali in addition to below Microsoft windows. Anyhow, you need to prepare a file system on a disk before you can mount it and this operation is called formatting. Instructions which includes mkfs.ext4 (in which mkfs stands for make filesystem) handle formatting. These instructions require, as a parameter, a tool record representing the partition to be formatted (as an example, /dev/sda1, the primary partition on the first drive). This operation is damaging and must be run handiest once, unless you want to wipe a filesystem and start clean.

There are also network filesystems which include NFS, which do no longer store statistics on a nearby disk. Instead, facts is transmitted through the community to a server that shops and retrieves them on demand. Thanks to the file system abstraction, you don't ought to fear about how this disk is attached, since the files continue to be available of their normal hierarchical manner.

3.4 Managing Progress

A procedure is a running example of a program, which requires memory to store both the program itself and its working records. The kernel is in fee of making and tracking processes. Whilst an application runs, the kernel first sets apart some reminiscence, hundreds the executable code from the record gadget into it, and then begins the code jogging. It keeps facts approximately this manner, the most visible of that's an identification wide variety called the process identifier (PID). Like most modern working systems, those with Unix like kernels, inclusive of Linux, are capable of multi-tasking. In different phrases, they permit the system to run many techniques at the same time. There's definitely only one going for walks procedure at someone time, however the kernel divides CPU time into small slices and runs each technique in flip. Due to the fact that these time slices are very quick (inside the millisecond range), they invent the advent of procedures walking in parallel, despite the fact that they may be lively handiest in the course of their time c language and are idle the relaxation of the time. The kernel's activity is to regulate its scheduling mechanisms to hold that appearance, while maximizing international system performance. If the time slices are too long, the utility may not appear as responsive as favored. Too quick, and the system loses time with the aid of switching duties too often. These choices may be subtle with processed priorities, wherein high precedence methods will run for longer durations and with greater common time slices than low priority approaches.

Multi-Processor System: The limitation described above, of handiest one process running at a time, doesn't usually apply: the actual limit is that there can be best one walking technique in step with processor middle. Multi-processor, multi core, or hyper threaded systems allow numerous methods to run in parallel. The equal time cutting system is used, although, to deal with cases in which there are more lively processes than to be had processor cores. This isn't always unusual: a simple system, even a typically idle one, nearly continually has tens of running processes.

The kernel permits several impartial times of the equal program to run, however every is authorized to get entry to handiest its very own time slices and memory. Their fact for that reason remains impartial.

3.5 Rights management

Unix like structures support multiple customers and agencies and allow control of permissions. Most of the time, a manner is recognized via the user who started out it. That technique is handiest accepted to take actions accepted for its owner. For example, starting a file requires the kernel to check the method identification towards get entry to permissions.

Chapter 4

4.1 Installation

4.2 Requirements for Installation

The installation requirements for Kali Linux vary depending on what you would like to install. At the low end, you can installation Kali as a simple at ease Shell (SSH) server with no computer, the usage of as little as 128 MB of RAM (512 MB endorsed) and 2 GB of disk space. At the higher quit, in case you choose to installation the default Xfce computing system and the kali Linux default metapackage, you ought to absolutely aim for at least 2048 MB of RAM and 20 GB of disk space. Besides the RAM and tough disk necessities, your pc needs to have a CPU supported via at the least one of the amd64, i386, or arm64 architectures.

4.3 Installation on a Hard Drive

On this segment, we count on which you have a bootable USB drive or DVD and which you booted from it to start the installation procedure.

4.4. Plain Installation

First, we can take a look at a standard Kali set up, with an unencrypted file system.

4.4.1 Booting and starting the Installer

As soon as the BIOS/UEFI has started booting from the USB force or DVD ROM, the iso Linux boot loader menu seems, as shown in determine 4.1, "Boot display screen" . At this stage, the Linux kernel is not but loaded; this menu lets in you to choose the kernel to boot and input optional parameters to be transferred to it inside the procedure. The usage of the arrow keys to do a fashionable installation, both pick out Graphical installation or deploy (for traditional textual content mode), then press the enter key to provoke the remainder of the setup procedure. Each menu entry hides a selected boot command line, which can be configured as wanted with the aid of pressing the Tab key before validating the access and booting.

Figure 4.1

Once booted, the setup program courses you step by step through the procedure. We can take a look at every of those steps in detail. We are able to cowl set up from a popular Kali Linux stay photo, installations from a mini. Iso may additionally appearance barely one of a kind. We are able to additionally cope with graphical mode set up, however the only difference from traditional textual content mode installation is the arrival. The variations pose equal questions and gift equal alternatives.

4.4.2 Selecting the Language

As shown in figure 4.2, "selecting the Language", the installation program starts in English, but the first step allows you to pick the language with a view to be used for the relaxation of the installation process. This language desire is also used to outline extra relevant default selections in subsequent levels (considerably the keyboard layout).

Navigating with the keyboard a few steps inside the setup procedure require you to go into statistics. Those displays

37

Have several regions which could gain focus (text access vicinity, checkboxes, listing of choices, ok and Cancel buttons), and the Tab key permits you to move from one to every other.

In graphical set up mode, you could use the mouse as you'll typically on an installed graphical desktop.

Figure 4.2

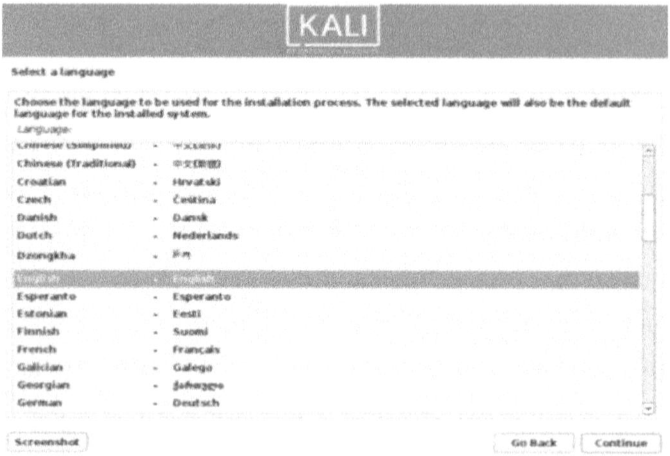

4.4.3 Selecting the Country

The second one step (Figure 4.3, "selecting the Country" is composed of choosing country. Blended with the language, this records enables the setup program to provide the most suitable keyboard format. This could additionally impact the configuration of the time sector. Inside the US, a Standard QWERTY keyboard is recommended, and the installer presents a choice of suitable time zones.

Figure 4.3

4.4.4 Selecting the Keyboard format

The proposed American English keyboard corresponds to the usual QWERTY layout as shown in Figure 4.4, "desire of Keyboard".

Figure 4.4

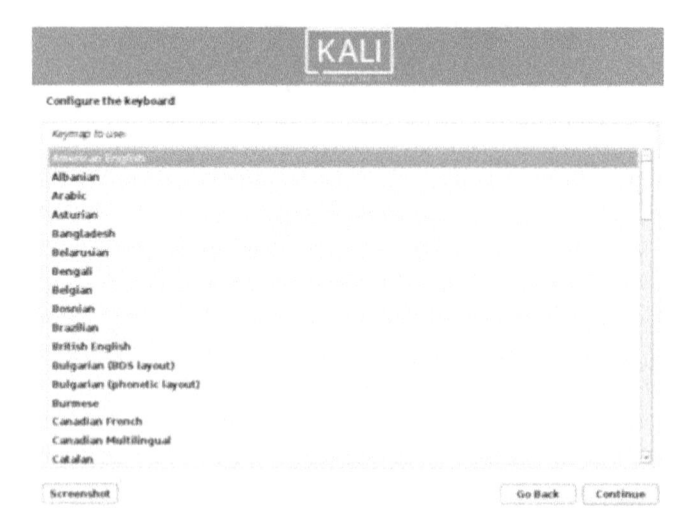

4.4.5 Detecting hardware

In the sizable majority of instances, the hardware detection step is completely computerized. The installer detects your hardware and tries to pick out the boot tool used which will get entry to its content. It loads the modules similar to the various hardware additives detected and then mounts the boot tool with the intention to examine it. The preceding steps have been absolutely contained inside the boot photo covered at the boot tool, a report of constrained length and loaded into memory with the aid of the bootloader when booting from the boot system.

4.4.6 Loading Components

With the contents of the boot system now to be had, the installer hundreds all the files essential to keep with its paintings. This consists of additional drivers for the final hardware (specifically the network card), in addition to all of the components of the installation application.

4.4.7 Detecting network hardware

In this step, the installer will try and automatically pick out the community card and cargo the corresponding module. If computerized detection fails, you can manually pick the module to load. If all else fails, you may load a particular module from a detachable system. This last solution is generally only wished if the best driving force isn't always covered within the standard Linux kernel, however, to be had somewhere else, including the manufacturer's website. This step should genuinely achieve success for community installations (inclusive of those finished when booting from a mini.iso), since the Debian applications must be loaded from the network.

4.4.8 Configuring the Network

As a way to automate the method as an awful lot as possible, the installer tries an automatic network configuration the use of Dynamic Host Configuration Protocol (DHCP) (for ipv4 and ipv6) and icmpv6's Neighbor Discovery Protocol (for ipv6), as proven in Figure , "network Autoconfiguration"

Figure 4.5

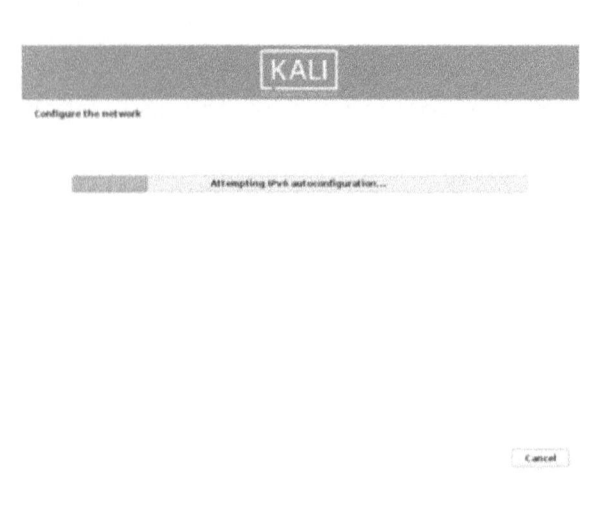

If the automatic configuration fails, the installer offers greater choices: attempt once more with a regular DHCP configuration, strive DHCP configuration by means of maintaining the call of the system, or installation a static community configuration.
This final choice requires an IP address, a subnet masks, an IP deal with for a capability gateway, a system name, and a site name.

4.4.9 user Creation

The installer prompts to create a new user (figure 4.6, "Create user") since it automatically creates a user account within the "sudo" organization. Which means the user has full administrative privileges via the sudo command. That is useful due to the reality that more than one objects are only to be had through administrative privileges. The installer also asks for a username for the account in addition to a password. The installer will request affirmation of the password to save you any input error.

Figure 4.6

> **KALI**
>
> Set up users and passwords
>
> A user account will be created for you to use instead of the root account for non-administrative activities.
>
> Please enter the real name of this user. This information will be used for instance as default origin for emails sent by this user as well as any program which displays or uses the user's real name. Your full name is a reasonable choice.
>
> Full name for the new user:
>
> kali user
>
> Screenshot   Go Back   Continue

4.4.10 Configuring the Clock

If the community is available, the system's internal clock could be updated from a network time protocol (NTP) server. This is useful because it ensures timestamps on logs may be correct from the first boot.

In case your country spans more than one time zones, you may be asked to pick the time zone that you want to apply, as proven in figure 4.7, "Time zone choice"

Figure 4.7

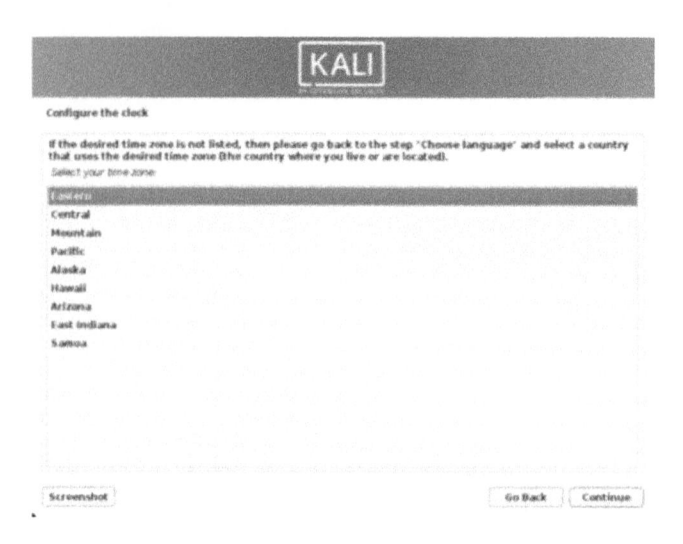

4.5 Detecting Disks and Other Systems

This step mechanically detects the difficult drives on which Kali may be installed, each of so that you can be presented inside the subsequent step: partitioning.

Partitioning

Partitioning is a critical step in installation, which consists of dividing the available space on the difficult drives into discrete sections (walls) consistent with the intended feature of the desktop and those walls. Partitioning also entails choosing the report systems for use. All of those decisions may have a power on performance, information safety, and server management.

The partitioning step is historically tough for new users. However, the Linux report systems and partitions, including virtual memory (or swap partitions) need to be described as they shape the foundation of the gadget. This project can end up complicated when you have already hooked up another working system at the gadget and also you want the two to coexist. In this situation, you should make certain not to regulate its walls, or if want be, resize them without causing damage. To house greater common (and less complicated) partition schemes, maximum customers will choose the Guided mode that recommends partition configurations and provides suggestions each step of the manner. More advanced users will respect the manual mode, which lets in for greater superior configurations. Every mode shares certain abilities.

Guided Partitioning the primary display in the partitioning system (figure 4.8, "choice of Partitioning Mode") presents entry points for the guided and guide partitioning modes. "Guided use whole disk" is the most effective and most not unusual partition scheme, so that you can allocate an entire disk to Kali Linux.

The following two choices use Logical volume manager (LVM) to set up logical (instead of physical), optionally encrypted, walls.

Eventually, the remaining choice initiates guide partitioning, which allows for greater advanced partitioning schemes, inclusive of installing Kali Linux alongside other running systems. In this example, we will allocate a whole tough disk to Kali, so we choose "Guided use complete disk" to proceed to the next step.

Figure 4.8

Partition disks

The installer can guide you through partitioning a disk (using different standard schemes) or, if you prefer, you can do it manually. With guided partitioning you will still have a chance later to review and customise the results.

If you choose guided partitioning for an entire disk, you will next be asked which disk should be used.

Partitioning method:

Guided - use entire disk
Guided - use entire disk and set up LVM
Guided - use entire disk and set up encrypted LVM
Manual

The subsequent display (proven in figure 4.9, "Disk to apply for Guided Partitioning" allows you to select the disk where Kali could be installed by means of deciding on the corresponding entry (for instance, "SCSI3 (0,0,0) (sda) 21.5 GB vmware, vmware virtual S"). Once decided on, guided partitioning will continue. This feature will erase all the statistics in this disk, so choose accurately.

Figure 4.9

Partition disks

Note that all data on the disk you select will be erased, but not before you have confirmed that you really want to make the changes.

Select disk to partition:

SCSI3 (0,0,0) (sda) - 21.5 GB VMware, VMware Virtual S

46

Subsequent, the guided partitioning system gives 3 partitioning techniques, which correspond to different usages, as proven in parent 4.10, "Guided Partition Allocation"

Figure 4.10

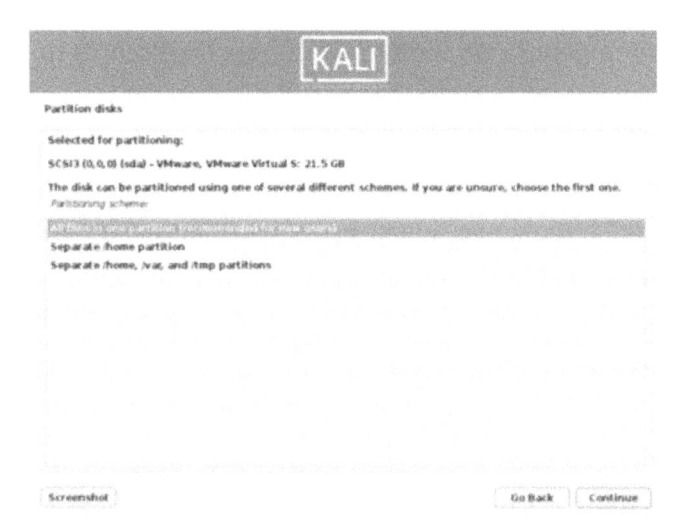

[KALI]

Partition disks

Selected for partitioning:
SCSI3 (0,0,0) (sda) - VMware, VMware Virtual S: 21.5 GB

The disk can be partitioned using one of several different schemes. If you are unsure, choose the first one.
Partitioning scheme:
All files in one partition (recommended for new users)
Separate /home partition
Separate /home, /var, and /tmp partitions

Screenshot   Go Back   Continue

The primary approach is known as "All files in one partition." The whole Linux system tree is saved in a single file system, similar to the root ("/") listing. This easy and strong partitioning scheme works flawlessly nicely for personal or single user structures. Despite the name, two walls will truly be created: the primary will house the complete gadget, the second the virtual reminiscence (or "swap"). The second one technique, "Separate /home/ temp partition," is comparable, however splits the record hierarchy in two: one partition contains the Linux system (/), and the second one incorporates "home directories" (meaning user facts, in files and subdirectories available under /home/). One benefit to this method is that it is simple to preserve the users' information when you have to reinstall the system. The remaining partitioning approach, known as "Separate /domestic, /var, and /temp partitions," is suitable for servers and multi user systems. It divides the record tree into many partitions: similarly, to the root (/) and user accounts (/home/) walls, it also has partitions for server software facts (/var/), and transient files (/temp/). One benefit to this method is that cease customers cannot lock up the server by using consuming all available difficult force area (they are able to only replenish /tmp/ and /domestic/). On the same time, service records (in particular logs) can now not clog up the rest of the system.

After choosing the form of partition, the installer presents a summary of your choices on the display screen as a partition map (figure 4.11, "Validating Partitioning") you could adjust every partition personally by means of selecting a partition. As an example, you can choose another record gadget if the usual (ext4) isn't suitable. In maximum cases, but the proposed partitioning is reasonable, and you may receive it by means of choosing "end partitioning and write modifications to disk." It may move without pronouncing, however pick out accurately as this will erase the contents of the chosen disk.

Figure 4.11

Chapter 5

5.1 Configuration of Kali Linux

5.2 Configuring the Network

In a standard desktop installation, you'll have Network Manager already set up and it is able to be controlled and configured through Xfce's system settings and via the top right menu as shown in figure 5.1, "Network Configuration system"

Figure 5.1

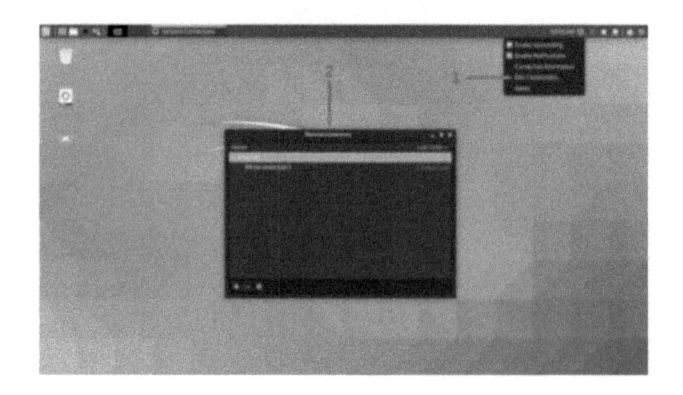

The default community configuration is predicated on DHCP to reap an IP deal with, DNS server, and gateway, but you can use the gear icon inside the lower left nook to regulate the configuration in many approaches (as an instance: set the MAC cope with, transfer to a static setup, enable or disable ipv6, and add additional routes). You could create profiles to save more than one wired network configurations and without problems transfer among them. For wireless networks, their settings are robotically tied to their public identifier (SSID). Network Manager also handles connections by means of mobile broadband (WIFI extensive region community WWAN) and by way of modems the use of on point protocol over ethernet (pppoe). Last but now not least, it offers integration with many sorts of virtual nonpublic networks (VPN) via committed plugins: SSH, open vpn, Cisco's VPNC, PPTP, Strong swan. Take a look at out the network manager* applications; most of them are not mounted by means of default.

5.2.1 On Command Line with Ifupdown

As an alternative, while you decide upon no longer to use (or don't have access to) a graphical desktop, you could configure the network with the already installed ifupdown package deal, which includes the ifup and ifdown tools. These tools examine definitions from the /and so forth/community/interfaces configuration report and are at the coronary heart of the /etc/init.d/networking init script that configures the network at boot time.

Every network device managed by using ifupdown may be de configured at any time with ifdown network device. You may then alter /and so forth/community/interfaces and produce the network again up (with the new configuration) with ifup network device.

Allow to take a look at what we are able to put in ifupdowns' configuration file. There are fundamental directives: automobile community device, which tells ifupdown to routinely configure the network interface once it is to be had, and iface network device inet/inet6 kind to configure a given interface.

```
auto lo                    # DHCP configuration
Iface lo inet loopback     #the loopback network interface
auto eth0                  #primary network interface
iface eth0 inet dhcp       #to get the ip
```

Notice that the special configuration for the loopback device need to constantly be found in this record. For a hard and fast IP address configuration, you need to provide greater information which includes the IP cope with, the network, and the IP of the gateway:

```
auto eth0            #primary network interface
Iface inet static
  address 192.168.1.18     #address
  netmask 255.255.255.0    #netmask
  broadcast 192.168.0.255  #broadcast
  network 192.168.0.0      #network
  gateway 192.168.1.1      #gateway
```

For WIFI interfaces, you should have the wpasupplicant package (included in Kali with the aid of default), which provides many wpa* alternatives that may be used in /etc/community/interfaces. Have a examine /usr/share/file/wpasupplicant/README.Debian.gz for examples and explanations. The most not unusual alternatives are wpa-ssid (which defines the name of the WIFI network to enroll in) and wpa psk (which defines the passphrase or the important thing protecting the community).

5.3 managing Unix users and Unix corporations

The database of Unix customers and companies includes the textual files /and so forth/passwd (list of customers), /etc/shadow (encrypted passwords of users), /and so forth/group (list of organizations), and /etc/gshadow (encrypted passwords of corporations). Their codecs are file in passwd(5), shadow(5), group(5), and gshadow(5) respectively while these files can be manually edited with gear like vipw and vigr, there are higher degree equipment to perform the most commonplace operations.

5.3.1 Creating User Accounts

Even though Kali is most often run at the same time as privileged with sudo permissions, you may regularly need to create unprivileged person bills for various reasons, specifically if you are using Kali as a primary operating machine. The most regular way to feature a user is with the adduser command, which takes a required argument: the username for the new user that you would like to create. The adduser command asks some questions earlier than creating the account but its usage is fairly honest. Its configuration record, /and so

52

on/adduser.conf, includes many thrilling settings. You could, for example, define the variety of user identifiers (uids) that can be used, dictate whether or no longer users share a common institution or no longer, outline default shells, and greater.

The advent of an account triggers the population of the user's domestic directory with the contents of the /etc/skel/ template. This offers the user with a fixed of popular directories and configuration files. In a few cases, it'll be beneficial to add a user to a group (apart from their default foremost institution) so that it will furnish extra permissions. For example, a person who's included in the docker institution has complete access to docker commands and services. This will be completed with a command including adduser person group.

5.3.2 Modifying an existing Account or Password

The subsequent commands permit modification of the statistics saved in precise fields of the person databases:

- Passwd—permits a regular user to change their password, which in flip, updates the /and so forth/ shadow file.
- Chfn—(change full name), reserved for the quality super user(root), modifies the GECOS, or "general records" field.
- Chsh—(change shell) changes the consumer's login shell. But to be had selections will be limited to those indexed in /and so forth/shells; the administrator, alternatively, is not bound with the aid of this limit and can set the shell to any software chosen.
- Chage—(alternate AGE) lets in the administrator to exchange the password expiration settings via passing the username as an argument or listing present day settings the use of the -l person choice. As an alternative, you could also force the expiration of a password the use of the passwd -e user

command, which forces the person to trade their password the subsequent time they log in.

5.3.3 Disabling an Account

You may find yourself needing to disable an account (lock out a person) as a disciplinary measure, for the purposes of a research, or sincerely in the occasion of an extended or definitive absence of a consumer. A disabled account means the user can't login or gain access to the machine. The account remains intact at the system and no files or information are deleted; it's far definitely inaccessible. That is done by means of the use of the command passwd -l user(lock). Re enabling the account is completed in comparable style, with the -u choice (unlock release).

5.3.4 Management of Unix Groups

The add group and delgroup instructions add or delete a group, respectively. The groupmod command modifies a collection's information (its gid or identifier). The command gpasswdgroup modifications the password for the group, while the gpasswd -r organization command deletes it.

5.4 Configuration of Specific Program

On this segment we can take a look at offerings (now and again referred to as daemons), or applications that run as a heritage method and carry out diverse functions for the device. We can begin through discussing configuration documents and could continue to provide an explanation for how some important offerings (inclusive of SSH, postgresql, and Apache) feature and the way they can be configured. Kali Linux's policy is to have any community services disabled by default, which is a distinctive conduct to different Linux working systems.

5.4.1 Configuring a Specific Software Program

When you want to configure an unknown package deal, you should proceed in stages. The/usr/share/document/package/README.Debian document is a good location to start. This document will often include statistics approximately the package, which include hints that may refer you to different documentation. You will regularly store yourself quite a few time, and avoid numerous frustration, by means of reading this record first because it frequently details the maximum commonplace mistakes and solutions to most not unusual troubles. Next, you need to take a look at the software program's authentic documentation.. The dpkg -L package deal command gives a listing of files blanketed within the package deal; you may therefore quick pick out the to be had documentation (as well as the configuration documents, located in /etc/). Additionally, dpkg -s bundle presentations the package deal meta facts and indicates any viable advocated or suggested packages; in there, you may find documentation or possibly a utility with a purpose to ease the configuration of the software program. Finally, the configuration files are often self-documented by way of many explanatory feedback eliminating the various possible values for each configuration putting. In a few instances, you could get software up and running via uncommenting a single line within the configuration document. In other cases, examples of configuration documents are furnished inside the /usr/proportion/doc/package/examples/ directory. They'll function a basis on your own configuration file.

5.4.2 Configuring SSH Remote Logins

SSH permits you to remotely log into a system, transfer files, or execute commands. It is an industry standard device (ssh) and provider (sshd) for connecting to machines remotely.

While the openssh server package is hooked up by way of default, the SSH service is disabled by means of default and for that reason isn't always started out at boot time. You could manually begin the SSH provider with systemctl start ssh or configure it to begin at boot time with systemctl allow ssh. The SSH provider has a surprisingly sane default configuration, but given its effective abilities and sensitive nature, it is right to know what you can do with its configuration file, /and so forth/ssh/sshd_ config.

5.4.3 Configuring postgresql Databases

Postgresql is a database server. It is hardly ever beneficial on its very own but is used by many different offerings to shop statistics. Those services will generally get right of entry to the database server over the network and usually require authentication credentials which will join. Putting in those services therefore requires developing postgresql databases and person accounts with appropriate privileges at the database. Which will do this, we need the carrier to be going for walks, so permit's begin it with systemctl start postgresql.

5.5 Type of Connection and Client Authentication

By default, postgresql listens for incoming connections in two ways: on TCP port 5432 of the local host interface and on report primarily based socket /var/run/postgresql/.s.PGSQL.5432. This can be configured in postgresql.conf with various directives: listen_addresses for the addresses to pay attention to, port for the TCP port, and unix_socket_directories to outline the listing where the record-based sockets are created.

Depending on how they join, clients are authenticated in extraordinary ways. The pg_hba.conf configuration report defines who is allowed to connect on each socket and how they're authenticated. By default, connections on the file-based socket use the Unix user account because the name of the postgresql user, and it assumes that not similarly authentication is needed. On the TCP connection, postgresql calls for the consumer to authenticate with a username and a password (though now not a Unix username/password but as an alternative one controlled by postgresql itself).The postgres user is special and has complete administrative privileges over all databases. We can use this identity to create new customers and new databases.

5.6 creating Users and Databases

The create user command provides a new person and drop user gets rid of one. Likewise, the createdb command adds a new database and dropdb eliminates one. Every of those instructions have their personal manual pages but we are able to talk a number of the options here. Every command acts at the default cluster (strolling on port 5432) but you can pass --port=port to modify customers and databases of a alternate cluster. These instructions have to connect to the postgresql server to do their task and that they must be authenticated as a consumer with enough privileges which will execute the desired operation.

5.7 Managing Postgresql Clusters

First, it is well worth noting that the concept of "postgresql cluster" is a Debian specific addition and that you may not find any reference to this time period inside the legit postgresql documentation. From the factor of view of the postgresql tools, this sort of cluster is just an instance of a database server jogging on a specific port.

That said, Debian's postgresql common package deal affords a couple of tools to manage such clusters: pg_createcluster, pg_dropcluster, pg_ctlcluster, pg_upgradecluster, pg_renamecluster, and pg_lsclusters. We won't cowl all those gear here, but you can seek advice from their respective guide pages for more information. What you should understand is that when a new main model of postgresql gets installed to your system, it's going to create a new cluster in an effort to run on the next port (commonly 5433) and you may hold the usage of the old model until you migrate your databases from the old cluster to the brand new one.

5.8 Configuring Apache

An ordinary Kali Linux installation consists of the Apache net server, supplied by the apache package. Being a community service, it is disabled through default. You may manually begin it with systemctl start apache. With increasingly applications being disbursed as internet programs, it is vital to have some understanding of Apache in order to host the ones programs, whether for local utilization or for making them to be had over the network.

Apache is a modular server, and many functions are applied by outside modules that the principal application hundreds during its initialization. The default configuration handiest permits the maximum not unusual modules, however enabling new modules is without difficulty finished by running a2enmod module. Use a2dismod module to disable a module. These programs definitely most effective create (or delete) symbolic links in /and so on/apache2/mods enabled/, pointing at the real files (saved in /and so forth/apache2/ mods to be had/). There are numerous modules available, however two are really worth initial consideration: php and SSL (used for TLS). Web programs written with php are completed by way of the Apache internet server with the assist of the committed module furnished by means of the libapache mod Hypertext Preprocessor bundle, and its set up routinely allows the module.

5.9 Service Management

Kali uses systemd as its init system, which is not only accountable for the boot series, but also permanently acts as a complete featured service manager, starting and monitoring services. Systemd can be queried and managed with systemctl. With no argument, it runs the systemctl list units command, which outputs a list of the active units. If you run systemctl fame, the output indicates a hierarchical assessment of the jogging offerings. Evaluating both out places, you straight away see that there are multiple forms of gadgets and that services are most effective considered one of them. Each service is represented by means of a service unit, that is defined by using a carrier document commonly shipped in /lib/systemd/device/ (or /run/systemd/gadget/, or /and many others/systemd/machine/; they're listed via increasing order of importance, and the final one wins). Each is likely modified by different carrier name.service.d/*.conf documents inside the same set of directories. The ones unit files are undeniable text documents whose layout is inspired by means of the known "*.ini" files of Microsoft windows, with key = fee pairs grouped between [segment] headers.

Chapter 6

6.1 Kali Linux: Securing and Monitoring

6.2 Security Policy

It is impractical to discuss security in vast strokes since the concept represents a huge range of concepts, tools, and tactics, none of which practice universally. Selecting amongst them requires a unique idea of what your desires are. Securing a gadget starts off evolved with answering some questions. Running headlong into imposing an arbitrary set of tools runs the hazard of focusing on the wrong components of protection. Additionally, it is best to determine a selected goal. A great method to assist with that dedication starts with the subsequent questions:

- What is the thing you want to protect? Security policy differs in sense what you want to secure computers or data. Inside the latter case, you furthermore might need to realize which records.
- What are you looking to defend against? Is it leakage of exclusive data and facts? Accidental loss of data? Loss of revenue because of disruption of service?
- Additionally, who are you looking to protect towards? Security features will be pretty distinct for guarding towards a typo through an everyday person of the gadget as opposed to defensive in opposition to a determined external attacker institution.

The time period "danger" is customarily used to refer together to these 3 factors: what to defend, what need to be avoided, and who may make this show up. Modeling the risk calls for solutions to those 3 questions. From this chance model, a safety coverage may be built, and the coverage can be implemented with concrete movements. More constraints are also well worth thinking of as they could restrict the range of available rules. How some distance are you willing to go to at ease a machine? This query has a primary impact on which coverage to put into effect. Too often, the solution is most effective described in terms of economic expenses, however other elements must also be considered, consisting of the quantity of inconvenience imposed on tools users or overall performance degradation.

As soon as the threat has been modeled, you may begin thinking about designing a real protection policy. There are extremes that may come into play when identifying the level of safety protections to undertake. On one hand, it can be extremely simple to provide basic system safety. As an instance, if the gadget to be covered handiest comprises a secondhand computer, the only use of which is to add some numbers on the end of the day, figuring out now not to do something special to defend it'd be quite affordable. The intrinsic value of the machine is low, and the value of the facts are zero given that they're not saved on the computer. A potential attacker infiltrating this device might only benefit a calculator. The price of securing one of these gadget might probably be more than the fee of a breach.

At the opposite give up of the spectrum, you might need to guard the confidentiality of mystery facts within the most complete manner possible, trumping another consideration. In this example, an appropriate response would be the overall destruction of the facts (securely erasing the files, shredding of the difficult disks to bits, then dissolving those bits in acid, and so forth). If there is a further requirement that facts should be kept in keep for future use (despite the fact that not necessarily comfortably available), and if value nonetheless isn't a factor, then a place to begin could be storing the information on iridium platinum alloy plates stored in bomb proof bunkers under numerous mountains inside the world, each of which being (of path) both entirely secret and protected by means of complete armies.

Extreme though these examples may additionally appear, they would nevertheless be a good enough response to certain described risks, insofar as they are the outcome of a concept manner that takes into consideration the dreams to reach and the limitations to satisfy. When coming from a reasoned selection, no safety coverage is greater, or less, first rate than some other.

Coming back to a more traditional case, a records device may be segmented into constant and typically independent subsystems. Every subsystem could have its personal requirements and constraints, and so the risk assessment and the layout of the safety policy ought to be undertaken one at a time for each. An excellent precept to preserve in mind is that a small attack surface is simpler to guard than a big one. The community organization must additionally be designed therefore: the touchy offerings should be targeting a small quantity of machines, and those machines have to only be accessible via a minimal quantity of routes or test factors. The common sense is straightforward: it's miles less difficult to comfortable those checkpoints than to relaxed all the touchy machines against everything of the outdoor international. It's miles at this factor that the usefulness of community filtering (which include by means of firewalls) becomes apparent. This filtering may be carried out with committed hardware, but an easier and greater flexible answer is to apply a software firewall such as the one integrated within the Linux kernel.

6.3 Possible Security Measures

As the preceding phase explained, there may be no unmarried reaction to the query of the way to comfortable Kali Linux. It all relies upon on how you operate it and what you are attempting to protect.

6.3.1 On a Server

If you run Kali Linux on a publicly accessible server, you maximum in all likelihood want to at secure network services by converting any default passwords that is probably configured. If you hand out user debts either without delay on the server or on one of the offerings, you need to make certain that you set sturdy passwords (they should withstand brute force assaults). At the identical time, you would possibly want to setup fail2ban, a good way to make it a lot harder to brute force passwords over the community (via filtering away IP addresses that exceed a restriction of failed login attempts). Installation fail2ban with apt replace followed through apt deploy fail2ban. In case you run web services, you probably need to host them over HTTPS to save you community intermediaries from sniffing your traffic (which would possibly encompass authentication cookies).

6.3.2 On a laptop

The computer of a penetration tester is not subject to the identical risks as a public server: as an instance, you are much less probable to be situation to random scans from script kiddies or even whilst you are, you possibly won't have any community offerings enabled.
Real threat often arises while you journey from one customer to the next. For instance, your computer will be stolen even as travelling or seized via customs. This is why you maximum possibly need to use full disk encryption and probable also setup the "nuke" the records that you have accrued for the duration of your engagements are confidential and require the maximum safety.
You could also want firewall policies but no longer for the same purpose as on the server. You might need to forbid all outbound traffic

except the traffic generated by means of your VPN access. This is supposed as a safety internet, so that after the VPN is down, you immediately notice it (instead of falling lower back to the nearby community get right of entry to). That manner, you do not disclose the IP addresses of your clients while you browse the internet or do different online activities. Similarly, in case you are performing a nearby inner engagement, it's far nice to remain on top of things of all of your pastime to lessen the noise you create at the community, that may alert the customer and their defense structures.

6.4 Securing Network Offerings

In general, it is a great idea to disable offerings that you do no longer use. Kali makes it easy to do this on the grounds that network offerings are disabled via default.

As long as services stay disabled, they do no longer pose any protection danger. But you need to be careful whilst you allow them because:

- There is no firewall by default, so if they listen on all network interfaces, they are effectively publicly to be had.
- A few offerings don't have any authentication credentials and assist you to set them on first use; others have default (and hence well known) credentials preset. Ensure to (re)set any password to something that best you know.
- Many services run as root with full administrator privileges, so the effects of unauthorized get entry to or a safety breach are consequently generally severe.

6.5 Firewall or Packet Filtering

A firewall is a chunk of computer system with hardware, software program, or each that parses the incoming or outgoing network packets (coming to or leaving from a nearby community) and most effective lets via the ones matching certain predefined situations.

A filtering community gateway is a form of firewall that protects an entire community. Additionally, it is established on a committed device configured as a gateway for the network so that it may parse all packets that skip inside and out of the network. As a substitute, a local firewall is a software provider that runs on one precise gadget so that it will clear out or restriction get admission to some services on that machine, or possibly to prevent outgoing connections with the aid of rogue software program that a person should, willingly or not, have mounted.

The Linux kernel embeds the netfilter firewall. There's no turnkey solution for configuring any firewall due to the fact that network and user requirements vary. But you can manipulate netfilter from user area with the iptables and ip6tables commands. The distinction among these two instructions is that the previous works for ipv4 networks, whereas the latter works on ipv6. Due to the fact that both network protocol stacks will in all likelihood be around for decades, both gear will want to be used in parallel. You could also use the splendid GUI based fwbuilder tool, which offers a graphical representation of the filtering regulations. But you make a decision to configure it, netfilter is Linux's firewall implementation, so let's take a closer observe how it works.

6.5.1 Netfilter behavior

Netfilter makes use of four distinct tables, which shop rules regulating 3 types of operations on packets:

- Filter out concerns filtering policies (accepting, refusing, or ignoring a packet).

- Nat (Network address Translation) issues translation of supply or destination addresses and ports of packets.
- Mangle issues other modifications to the IP packets (including the tos form of service field and options).
- Raw permits different manual modifications on packets earlier than they reach the relationship tracking system.

Each table includes lists of guidelines known as chains. The firewall uses standard chains to deal with packets based on predefined circumstances. The administrator can create other chains, if you want to simplest be used while referred through certainly one of the standard chains (either without delay or circuitously).
The filter table has three known chains:

- INPUT: issues packets whose vacation spot is the firewall itself.
- OUTPUT: concerns packets emitted through the firewall.
- Ahead: concerns packets passing through the firewall (which is neither their source nor their destination).

The Nat desk also has three popular chains:
- PREROUTING: to modify packets as quickly as they come.
- POSTROUTING: to modify packets whilst they are ready to go on their way.
- OUTPUT: to alter packets generated by using the firewall itself.

These chains are illustrated in figure 6.1, "How Netfilter Chains are referred to as"

Figure 6.1

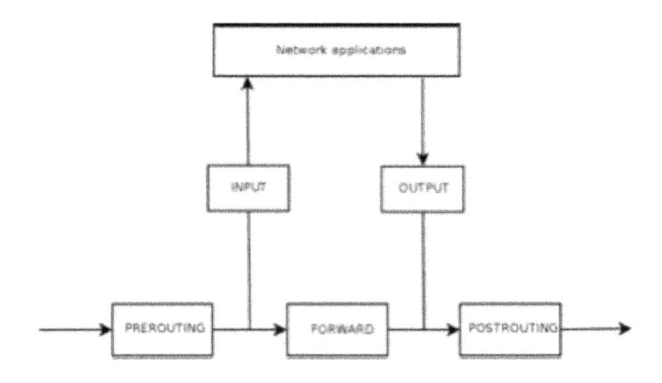

Every chain is a listing of regulations; every rule is a hard and fast of situations and an action to perform when the situations are met. Whilst processing a packet, the firewall scans the right chain, one rule after some other, and when the conditions for one rule are met, it jumps to the desired movement to preserve processing. The most commonplace behaviors are standardized, and dedicated moves exist for them. Taking this sort of standard actions interrupts the processing of the chain, since the packets fate is already sealed (barring an exception mentioned under). Indexed below are the Netfilter movements.

- **ACCEPT**: allow the packet to move on its way.
- **REJECT:** reject the packet with a web manipulate message protocol (ICMP) error packet
- (the --reject-with kind choice of iptables determines the kind of error to ship).
- **DROP:** delete (ignore) the packet.
- **LOG:** log (via syslog) a message with an outline of the packet. Be aware that this action does now not interrupt processing, and the execution of the chain maintains at the following rule, which is why logging refused packets requires each a LOG and a REJECT/DROP rule. Common parameters related to logging include:

- o --log-level, with default value warning, indicates the syslog severity level.
- o --log-prefix allows specifying a textual content prefix to distinguish among logged messages.
- o --log-tcp-sequence, --log-tcp-options, and --log-ip-options indicate extra records to be integrated into the message: respectively, the TCP sequence quantity, TCP options, and IP alternatives.

- **ULOG:** log a message through ulogd, which may be higher adapted and greater efficient than syslogd for managing huge numbers of messages; be aware that this movement, like LOG, also returns processing to the following rule inside the calling chain.
- **Chain_name:** jump to the given chain and compare its policies.
- **RETURN:** interrupt processing of the cutting-edge chain and return to the calling chain; in case the modern chain is a preferred one, there's no calling chain, so the default motion (defined with the -P choice to iptables) is achieved alternatively.
- **SNAT** (only within the Nat table): practice supply community address Translation (SNAT). Extra options describe the exact adjustments to apply, such as to the source cope with port option, which defines the new supply IP address and/or port.
- **DNAT** (most effective within the nat table): practice vacation spot community deal with Translation (DNAT). Greater options describe the exact adjustments to use, which includes to the destination cope with port choice, which defines the new destination IP cope with and/or port.
- **MASQUERADE** (only in the nat table): apply masquerading (a special case of supply NAT).
- **REDIRECT** (simplest in the nat table): transparently redirect a packet to a given port of the firewall itself; this will be used to set

up a transparent web proxy that works and not using a configuration on the client side, for the reason that consumer thinks it connects to the recipient while the communications absolutely undergo the proxy. To the ports port(s) choice suggests the port, or port range, where the packets need to be redirected.

6.5.2 Syntax of iptables and ip6tables

The iptables and ip6tables commands are used to control tables, chains, and guidelines.
Their -t table option suggests which table to perform on (by way of default, filter out).

Commands

The main alternatives for interacting with chains are indexed underneath:

- -L chain lists the policies inside the chain. That is commonly used with the -n choice to disable name resolution (for instance, iptables -n -L input will show the rules related to in- coming packets).
- -N chain creates a new chain. New chains can be made for multiple purposes, such as checking out a new network carrier or averting a community attack.
- -X chain deletes an empty and unused chain (as an example, iptables -X ddos-attack).
- -A chain rule provides a rule at the give up of the given chain. Take into account that guidelines are processed from top to bottom so be sure to keep this in thoughts when including regulations.
- -I chain rule_num inserts a rule right before the rule number rule_num. As with the -A option, maintain the processing order in thoughts whilst placing new guidelines into a series.

- -D chain rule_num(or -D chain rule) it deletes the rule present in a chain: the very first syntax identifies the rule to be deleted by its wide variety (iptables -L –line numbers will show those numbers), at the same time as the latter identifies it by using its contents.
- -F chain flushes a sequence (deletes all its policies). As an instance, to delete all the guidelines associated with outgoing packets, you'll run iptables -F OUTPUT. If no chain is stated, all of the policies in the table are deleted.
- -P chain defines the action which is default action, or some "policy" for any given chain it is important to note that only standard chains may have such a coverage. To drop all incoming site visitors via default, you would run iptables -P enter DROP.

Rules

Every rule is expressed as situations -j action action_options. If several situations are described in the identical rule, then the criterion is the conjunction (logical AND) of the conditions, that is at least as restrictive as every person circumstance.

The -p protocol condition suits the protocol subject of the IP packet. The maximum not unusual values are tcp, udp, icmp, and icmpv6. This condition can be complemented with situations at the TCP ports, with clauses consisting of –support -port port and –destination-port port.

6.5.3 Creating Rules

Each rule introduction calls for one invocation of iptables or ip6tables. Typing these commands manually can be tedious, so the calls are commonly stored in a script in order that the device is automatically configured the same manner whenever the device boots. This script may be written through hand however it is able to additionally be thrilling to put together it with an excessive degree tool together with fwbuilder. The principle is straightforward. In the first step, describe all of the factors on the way to be concerned within the actual regulations:

- Servers
- with its network interfaces, the firewall itself
- with the corresponding IP ranges, the network
- belonging ports to the services only hosted on the servers

Then the action wishes to be selected and configured. As far as ipv6 is concerned, you could both create distinct rulesets for ipv4 and ipv6, or create most effective one and allow fwbuilder translate the regulations in step with the addresses assigned to the items. Fwbuilder will generate a script configuring the firewall according to the policies which you have defined. Its modular structure offers it the capability to generate scripts targeting distinctive structures along with iptables for Linux, ipf for freebsd, and pf for OpenBSD.

Figure 6.2

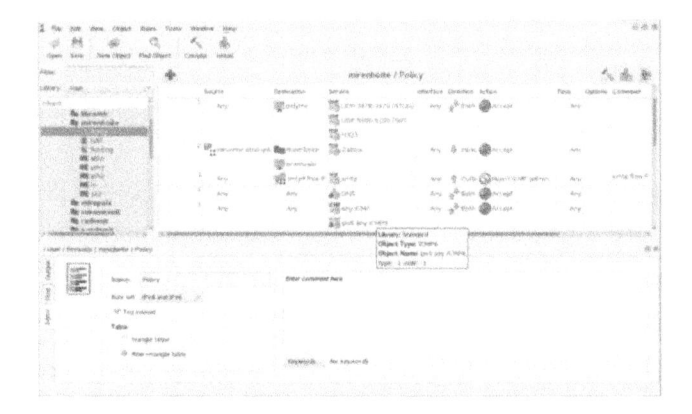

6.5.4 Installing in the rules at every Boot

So that you can put into effect the firewall rules on every occasion the machine is booted, you will want to sign in the configuration script in an up directive of the /and so forth/community/interfaces document. Within the following example, the script is stored under /usr/nearby/etc/awais.fw (awais being the hostname of the machine).

```
Auto eth0              #primary network interface
Iface inet static
 Address 192.168.1.18      #address
 Netmask 255.255.255.0   #netmask
 Broadcast 192.168.0.255 #broadcast
 Network 192.168.0.0       #network
 Gateway 192.168.1.1       #gateway
 Up/usr/nearby/etc/awais.fw
```

This case assumes which you are using ifupdown to configure the network interfaces. In case you are the use of something else (like network manager or systemd-networkd), then refer to their respective documentation to discover ways to execute a script after the interface has been added up.

6.6 Logging and Monitoring

Data confidentiality and protection is a crucial thing of safety, but it is similarly critical to ensure availability of offerings. As an administrator and safety practitioner, you have to ensure that the whole lot works as expected, and it is your obligation to locate anomalous behavior and provider degradation in a timely way. Tracking and logging software plays a key function on this component of security, imparting perception into what's happening on the system and the network. In this segment, we can evaluation a few equipment that may be used to reveal several components of a Kali gadget.

6.6.1 monitoring Logs with logcheck

The logcheck application monitors log files each hour by way of default and sends unusual log messages in emails to the administrator for further analysis. The listing of monitored documents is stored in /etc/logcheck/logcheck.logfiles. The default values
Paintings excellent if the /and so forth/rsyslog.conf file has no longer been absolutely overhauled. Logcheck can report in numerous degrees of element: paranoid, server, and notebook. Paranoid is very verbose and should likely be constrained to unique servers which include firewalls. Server is the default mode and is recommended for maximum servers. Notebook is obviously designed for workstations and is extremely terse, filtering out greater messages than the opposite options. In all three cases, logcheck must probably be customized to exclude some greater messages (depending on set up offerings), except you actually need to receive hourly batches of lengthy uninteresting emails. Because the message choice mechanism is as an alternative complex, /usr/share/document/ logcheck database/README.logcheck database.gz is a required if difficult study.

6.6.2 Monitoring Interest in Real Time

Top is an interactive device that shows a listing of currently running approaches. The default sorting is based on the contemporary amount of processor use and can be acquired with the P key. Different sort orders consist of a sort by occupied reminiscence (M key), by way of general processor time (T key), and by way of method identifier (N key). The k key kills a process via coming into its method identifier. The r key modifications the priority of a manner. When the gadget appears to be overloaded, top is an incredible tool to see which approaches are competing for processor time or consuming an excessive amount of memory. Mainly, it's miles frequently thrilling to check if the methods ingesting resources healthy the actual offerings that the machine is thought to host. An unknown system walking because the "www - records" consumer ought to virtually stand out and be investigated since it's likely an example of software established and completed at the system thru a vulnerability in a web utility. Top is a completely flexible device, and its manual web page offers information on the way to customize its display and adapt it to your private desires and habits. The xfce4v task manager graphical tool is just like pinnacle and it affords roughly the equal features. For GNOME users there is gnome system screen and for KDE users there is ksysguard which can be each comparable as nicely.

Conclusion

Congratulations you have done tremendous and have learnt much about Kali Linux system. And you should use it in various projects to get hold of the knowledge. You have discovered and learnt interesting features of Kali Linux and know that they have some limitations, and you need to work around those limitations. With constantly changing distributions and boost of technology everyday some part of the book become older, so you need to keep up with the knowledge.

LINUX

© Copyright 2021 by - All rights reserved.

This document is geared towards providing exact and reliable information in regards to the topic and issue covered. The publication is sold with the idea that the publisher is not required to render accounting, officially permitted, or otherwise, qualified services. If advice is necessary, legal or professional, a practiced individual in the profession should be ordered.

- From a Declaration of Principles which was accepted and approved equally by a Committee of the American Bar Association and a Committee of Publishers and Associations.

In no way is it legal to reproduce, duplicate, or transmit any part of this document in either electronic means or in printed format. Recording of this publication is strictly prohibited and any storage of this document is not allowed unless with written permission from the publisher. All rights reserved.

The information provided herein is stated to be truthful and consistent, in that any liability, in terms of inattention or otherwise, by any usage or abuse of any policies, processes, or directions contained within is the solitary and utter responsibility of the recipient reader. Under no circumstances will any legal responsibility or blame be held against the publisher for any reparation, damages, or monetary loss due to the information herein, either directly or indirectly.

Respective authors own all copyrights not held by the publisher.

The information herein is offered for informational purposes solely and is universal as such. The presentation of the information is without a contract or any type of guarantee assurance.

The trademarks that are used are without any consent, and the publication of the trademark is without permission or backing by the trademark owner. All trademarks and brands within this book are for clarifying purposes only and are owned by the owners themselves, not affiliated with this document.

Introduction

Linux
Linux is a famous, opensource computer program environment that competes with Microsoft windows and the Apple Macintosh. It has 4 fundamental elements:

The kernel
The low-level running system, handling files, disks, internet working, and different requirements we take as granted.

Supplied programs
Heaps of applications for document manipulation, textual content editing, arithmetic, typesetting, audio, video, laptop programming, internet web page creation, encryption, CD burning You name it.

The shell
A person interface for typing instructions, executing them, and displaying the consequences. There are various shells in lifestyles: the Bourne shell, Korn shell, C shell, and others. This book focuses on bash, the Bourne again Shell, that is frequently the default for user money owed. But some of these shells have similar basic features.

X

A graphical system that provides windows, menus, icons, mouse support, and other familiar GUI elements. More complex graphical environments are built on X; the most popular are KDE and GNOME. Throughout this book, we discuss programs that open their own X windows to run.

Chapter 1

1.1 Fedora Linux

Fedora Linux is one specific Linux distribution or "distro," created through crimson Hat, Inc. And the Fedora undertaking (for more and the Fedora task (for extra statistics, see http://fedora.redhat.com) and formerly known as red Hat Linux.* Our material is primarily based on Fedora core 1, the first professional launch (November 2003). We focus on the supplied packages and the shell, with short insurance of X and the kernel as wanted.

1.2 Command

A Linux command typically consists of an application name followed by options and arguments, typed within a shell. The program call refers to an application someplace on disk (which the shell will discover and run). Options, which normally begin with a sprint, have an effect on the behavior of the program, and arguments generally constitute inputs and outputs. For example, this command to count number the lines in a file:

$ wc l my_file

Includes a program (wc, the "word count" program), an option (l) saying to count lines, and an argument (my_file) indicating the report to study. (The dollar signal is a spark off from the shell, indicating that it is waiting for your command.) Alternatives can be given individually:

$ my_program a b c my_file   three person options

Or mixed behind a single dash:

$ my_program abc my_file   same as a b c

Even though some applications are quirky and do not apprehend combined options.

Commands can also be a great deal more complicated than jogging a single application:

- They could run numerous packages without delay, either in sequence (one after the other) or linked right into a "pipeline" with the output of one command becoming the input of the subsequent.

Red Hat now specializes in its organization Linux merchandise for higher end applications. Maximum of this book applies to corporation and other Linux distros.

- Options are not standardized. The same option (say, l) might also have specific meanings to exceptional packages: in wc l it method "count strains of textual content," however in ls l it manner "produce longer output." Within the other direction, two seasoned grams would possibly use unique options to mean the same issue, together with q for "run quietly" versus s for "run silently."
- Likewise, arguments are not standardized. They often represent filenames for enter or output, but they can be other things too, like directory names or everyday expressions.
- The Linux command line person interface the shell has a programming language constructed in. So as opposed to a com mand announcing "run this application," it had a say, "if nowadays is Tuesday, run this application, in any other case run every other com mand six times for every document whose name leads to .txt."

1.3 Users & Superusers

Linux is a multiuser operating machine. On a given pc, each user is identified by way of a unique username, like "ben" or "funky guy," and owns a (fairly) personal part of the system for doing paintings. There's also a specifically specific user, with username root, who has the privileges to do something in any respect at the device. Normal users are confined: even though they could run most applications, in known they could regulate handiest the files they personal. The superuser, alternatively, can create, regulate, or delete any record and run any software. Some commands on this book can be run efficaciously only through the superuser. In this situation, we use a hash mark (#) because the shell activate:

command goes right here

Otherwise, we are able to use the dollar sign spark off indicating an ordinary user:

$ command goes right here

To grow to be the superuser, you needn't log out and log again in; simply run the su command and provide the superuser password:

$ su l
Password: *****#

Chapter 2

When we describe a command, we first present its general utilization facts. For example, the wc (word matter) seasoned gram has the overall usage:

wc [options] [files]   general usage

Which means you'd type "wc" followed, if you pick, by using options and then filenames. You wouldn't type the rectangular brackets "[" and "]": they just imply their contents are elective; and phrases in italics suggest you have to fill for your very own precise values, like names of actual documents. In case you see a vertical bar among alternatives or arguments, possibly grouped by using parentheses:

ls (file | directory)   indicates choice

This shows desire: while going for walks the ls command, you may also deliver either a report or listing name as a controversy.

2.1 Input and Output

Most Linux applications receive information from trendy enter, which is normally your keyboard, and bring output on general output, which is generally your screen. Moreover, mistakes messages are typically displayed on trendy errors, which is also commonly your display screen but stored break free popular output.* Later we'll see a way to redirect popular input, output, and error to and from documents or pipes. But let's get our vocabulary directly. When we say a command "reads," we imply from standard input until we are saying in any other case. And when a com mand "prints," we mean on fashionable output, except we're talking about pc printers.

2.2 Standard heading

Each command description starts with a heading like this one for the ls (listing files) command.

2.2.1 ls [options] [files]

The heading consists of the command call (ls) and usage, the directory in which it's miles placed (/bin), the RPM package deal that set up the command (coreutils), and six properties of the command printed in black (supported) or gray (unsupported):

2.2.2 Stdin
The command reads from known input, i.e., your keyboard, through default.

2.2.3 Stdout
The command writes to conventional output, i.e., your screen, through default.

2.2.4 File

In case you supply a sprint () argument in area of an input document call, the command reads from fashionable input; and also, if the dash is furnished as an output filename, the command writes to traditional output. For instance, the following wc (word be counted) command line reads the documents file1 and file2, then preferred enter, then file3:

$ wc file_1 file_2 file_3

2.2.5. Opt

If you supply the command line choice "" it approach "end of options": something performing in a while the command line isn't always a choice. That is now and again vital to operate on a record whose name starts with a sprint, which otherwise would be (mistakenly) handled as an option. For example, when you have a record named foo, the command wc foo will fail due to the fact foo will be treated as an (invalid) alternative. Wc foo works. If a command does no longer guide "", you could prepend the modern day. Listing path "./" to the filename so the sprint is not the first person:

$ wc ./foo

2.2.6 Help

The option assist makes the command print an assist message explaining right usage, then exit.
Version
The choice version makes the command print its model quantity and go out.

2.2.7 Standard symbols

In the course of the book, we use certain symbols to indicate keystrokes. Like many different Linux documents, we use the ^ symbol to mean "press and hold the control (Ctrl) key," so as an instance, ^D (mentioned "control D") approach "press and hold the control key and type D." We also write ESC to intend "press the Esc key." Keys like enter and Spacebar must be explanatory.

2.2.8 The echo command, your friend

In a lot of our examples, we'll print facts to the display with the echo command, which we'll formally describe in "screen Output". Echo is one of the most effective commands: it simply prints its arguments on known out placed, as soon as those arguments were processed by way of the shell.

```
$ echo I am a Linux programmer
I am a Linux programmer
$ echo My name is $user
My name is ben
```

2.3 Getting the Help

If you want greater data than this book offers, there are several matters you may do.

2.3.1 Run the man command

The man command shows a web guide web page, or manual, for a given application. As an example, to get documentation on listing documents with ls, run:

```
$ man ls         to display the online manual page
```

To search for manpages by keyword for a specific subject matter, use the k option followed by the keyword:

```
$ man k keyword
```

2.3.2 Run the info command

The data command is a prolonged, hypertext assist system protecting many Linux packages.

$ info ls.   To help cover many Linux programs

If no documentation is determined on a given program, information shows this system's manpage. For a listing of available documentation, type data by itself. To discover ways to navigate the info device, kind info information.

2.3.3 Use the help option (if any)

Many Linux commands respond to the option assist with the aid of printing a short assist message. Try:

$ ls –help   displays the help message

2.3.4 Examine the directory /usr/share/doc

This listing consists of assisting files for lots of packages, commonly organized by way of application call and version. As an example, documents for the textual content editor Emacs, Version 21.5, are located in /usr/proportion/doc/emacs21.5.

2.4 GNOME and KDE help

For assist with GNOME or KDE, pick out the assist item within the main menu.

Fedora specific internet sites

The official website online is http://fedora.redhat.com. An unofficial FAQ has sprung up at http://fedora.artoo.net. And of direction there's the net website online for this e book:
Http://www.oreilly.com/catalog/linuxpg/

2.4.1 Usenet newsgroups

Usenet has dozens of newsgroups on Linux subjects, consisting of comp.os.linux.misc and comp.os.linux.questions. For Red Hatspecific data, try alt.os.linux.redhat, comp.os.linux.redhat, linux.redhat, and linux.redhat.misc. You could seek via newsgroup postings at Google groups, http://agencies.google.com, which is a goldmine of troubleshooting facts.

2.4.2 Google

Search Google for further documentation and tutorials at http://www.google.com (if you've been residing in a closet).

2.4.3 Fedora: a primary View

While you log right into a Fedora (or different) Linux machine, you're in all likelihood to be greeted through a graphical desktop like determine 1, which includes:

- A home windows like taskbar across the lowest, with:
  - A "pink hat" icon in the lower left, which when clicked, pops up a firstrate menu of packages
  - Icons to run diverse packages, inclusive of the Mozilla net browser, Evolution electronic mail program, and Print manager for configuring printers
  - A computer switcher (the square with 4 boxes in it), which lets you hold and switch between multiple desktops
  - A blue checkmark indicating that your device tender ware is updated, or a purple exclamation factor warning you that it isn't
  - A clock

- Other icons on the computer, such as a trash can for deleting documents, a floppy disk, and your house directory (folder) for storing nonpublic files

Figure 1.1

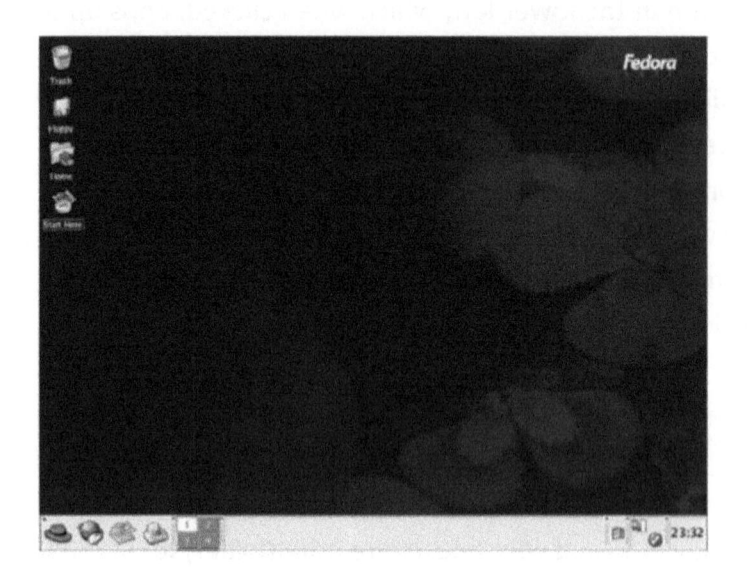

Fedora comes with several similar interfaces, and the one you're viewing is either GNOME or KDE.* you could inform the distinction through clicking the crimson hat icon to bring up the main menu and choosing Help. The assist window that appears will without a doubt suggest GNOME or KDE.

Chapter 3

3.1 Role of the shell

Explore the environment of icons and menus in GNOME and KDE. Those graphical interfaces are, for some users, the number one way to compute with Linux. Various distros, including Fedora, simplify those interfaces so users can edit files, read electronic mail, and read the net without much effort. Nevertheless, the true energy of Linux lies behind the curtain. To get the maximum out of Linux, you ought to come to be proficient in the use of the shell. It would start with be more difficult than icons and menus, but once you're used to it, the shell is quite clean to use and very powerful. Maximum of this book discusses Linux instructions run through the shell.

3.1.1 How to run a shell

To run a shell within GNOME, KDE, or another graphical interface for Linux, you will want to open a shell window. This is done by way of applications like xterm, gnome terminal, konsole, and uxterm. Each of these programs does the same simple component: open a window that is strolling a shell, watching for your input. To run a shell window the usage of the three default windowing interfaces for Fedora:

Interfaces window programs	Take this action
GNOME desktop:	Menu : System of Tools : on the Terminal or on the gnome terminal
	Right Mouse Button : Open up the Terminal

KDE   Menu : System of Tools : on the Terminal or on the desktop: konsole

        Right Mouse Button : Open Terminal

Twm   on the desktop:

xterm

        Right Mouse Button : xterm

Do not confuse the window program(like konsole) with the shell running interior it. The window is just a field albeit with fancy capabilities of its personal, but the shell is what prompts you for commands and runs them. If you're now not running a graphical interface say, you are logging in remotely over the community, or directly over a connected terminal a shell will run at once while you log in. No shell window is needed.

Chapter 4

4.1 Shutdowns, logins and logouts

We assume you already know the way to log into your Linux account. To log out from GNOME or KDE, click the crimson hat icon within the taskbar and choose Logout from the main menu. To sign off from a remote shell, simply close the shell (type exit or logout). By no means genuinely flip off the power to a Linux device: it needs a sleek shutdown. To perform a shutdown from GNOME, select Logout → close Down. From KDE, first sign off, then on the login display screen, click on the Shutdown icon. To perform a shutdown from a shell, run the shutdown command because the superuser, as follows.

4.2 Shutdowns

The shutdown command halts or reboots a Linux machine; handiest the superuser can also run it. Here's a command to halt the gadget in 5 mins, broadcasting the message "scheduled protection" to all users logged in:

shutdown h +5 " the scheduled maintenance of system"

The time can be some of mins preceded via a plus sign, like +5, an absolute time in hours and minutes, like 16:25, or the phrase now to mean at once. Without a alternatives, shutdown places the device into single person mode, a unique maintenance mode wherein only one character is logged in (at the gadget console), and all nonessential offerings are off. To go out single user mode, either perform another shutdown to halt or reboot, or type ^D to deliver up the system in regular, multiuser mode.

Useful options to use

- R to Reboot the device.
- H to Halt the device.
- K   Kidding: don't surely carry out a shutdown, just broadcast warning messages to all users as if the device had been going down.
- C. Cancel a shutdown in development (omit the time argument)
- F on reboot, pass the same old filesystem test achieved by using the fsck program
- F on reboot, require the standard filesystem check.

For technical records about shutdowns, single user mode, and various machine states, see the manpages for init and inittab.

Chapter 5

5.1 Filesystem

To utilize any Linux system, you need to be consolation capable with Linux files and their layout. Every Linux document is contained in a set referred to as a directory. Directories are like folders on windows and Macintosh structures. Directories form a hierarchy, or tree: one listing may include different directories, known as subdirectories, which might also themselves contain different files and subdirectories, and so forth, into infinity. The topmost directory is known as the root listing and is denoted by using a lessen (/). We seek advice from files and directories using a "names and slashes" syntax known as a path. As an instance, this path:

/one/two/three/four/five..

Refers to the root directory /, which contains a listing referred to as one, which includes a directory , which contains a listing three, which includes a final file or listing, four. If a route starts with the basis directory, it's known as an absolute path, and if now not, it's a relative course. Greater in this in a moment. On every occasion you're going for walks a shell, that shell is "in" a few directory (in a summary experience). Extra technically, your shell has a currently operating listing, and while you run instructions in that shell, they operate relative (there's that phrase again) to the directory. Greater especially, if you check with a relative file course in that shell, it's miles relative on your contemporary running directory. As an example, in case your shell is "in" the directory /one/two/three, and you run a command that refers to a record my_file, then it's virtually /one/two/three/four/my_file. Likewise, a relative path a/b/c might suggest the true course /one/two/three/four/a/b/c/d. Unique directories are denoted. (a single period) and (two periods in a row). The former method your currently directory, and the latter method your discern directory, one level above. So, if your modern listing is /one/two/three/four, then. Refers to this listing and .. Refers to /one/two/thee.

You "move" your shell from one directory to any other the use of the cd command:

$ cd /one/two/three   to move the directory from one to other

More technically, this command changes your shell's present day working directory to be /one/two/three. That is an absolute alternate (because the listing begins with "/"); of route you can make relative movements as nicely:

$ cd d	input subdirectory d
$ cd ../my_dir	go up to my parent, then into listing my_dir

File and directory names may additionally comprise most characters you anticipate capital and small letters, numbers, intervals, dashes, underscores, and most other symbols (just now not "/"; it's reserved for isolating directories). In standard, however, keep away from using areas, asterisks, parentheses, and other characters which have unique that means to the shell. Otherwise, you'll need to quote or break out these characters all of the time.

5.2 Home Directories

Users' private files are often discovered in /home (for regular users) or /root (for superusers). Your own home directory is usually /home/username: /home/ben, /home/ben, and so on. There are several approaches to locate or refer from your home directory.

Cd

Without an arguments, the cd command returns you (i.e., units the shell's running listing) to your property directory.

5.3 HOME Directories

The environment variable home includes the name of your own home listing.

$ echo $Home   the echo command prints the arguments
/home/ben

~

While utilized in place of a listing, a lone tilde is expanded with the aid of the shell to the name of your house directory.

$ echo ~
/home/ben

When followed by a username (as in ~ben), the shell expands this string to be the hom domestic directory:

$ cd ~ben
$ pwd
/home/ben

5.4 System Directories

A typical Linux machine has tens of heaps of device directories. Those directories comprise working machine files, applications, documentation, and pretty much the whole thing except nonpublic person files (which commonly live in /domestic).
Until you're a machine administrator, you'll rarely visit maximum device directories however with a little expertise you may apprehend

or wager their functions. Their names regularly contain three elements, which we'll name the scope, category, and application. (those are not fashionable terms, but they'll assist you recognize things.) As an example, the listing /usr/nearby/ percentage/emacs, which includes nearby information for the Emacs text editor, has scope /usr/local (domestically established gadget files), category share (software specific information and documentation), and alertness emacs (a text editor), shown in figure five.1. We'll give an explanation for those three components, barely out of order.

Figure 5.1

/usr/local/share/emacs
 Scope   Category   Application

Directory path part 1: category

A category tells you the varieties of files found in a directory. As an example, if the class is bin, you can be reasonably confident that the listing contains applications. Not unusual categories are indexed below.

5.5 Categories for programs

Bin   programs (normally binary files)
Sbin   programs (commonly binary files) meant to be run by using the superuser, root
Lib   Libraries of code utilized by programs
Libexec   programs invoked by different programs, no longer normally by using users;   suppose "library of executable applications"

5.6 Categories for documentation

Doc Documentation
Info Documentation files for Emacs's integrated assist system
Man Documentation files (manual pages) displayed by way of the man program; the files are often compressed, or sprinkled with typesetting instructions for man to interpret.
Share program specific documents, along with examples and set up instructions

5.7 Categories for configuration

Etc Configuration documents for the device (and other miscellaneous stuff)
Init.d Configuration files for booting Linux; also, rc1.d, rc2.d, ...
Rc.d

5.8 Classes for programming

Include Header documents for programming
Src source code for packages

5.9 Categories for web files

cgi-bin Scripts/programs that run on internet pages
html web pages
public_html web pages, commonly in users' domestic directories
www web pages

5.10 Categories for display

X11. X window gadget documents
fonts fonts(wow! Har to guess)

5.11 Categories for hardware

Mnt Mount point: directories that provide get admission to disks
Misc
Dev device files for interfacing with disks and other hardware

5.12 Categories for runtime files

Lock it Locks the files, created with the aid of applications to say, "I am strolling and running;" the existence of a lock document may prevent some other program, or another example of the equal program, from running or performing an action
Var files precise to this computer, created and updated because the pc runs
Log the Log documents that track vital device events, containing errors, caution, and informational messages
Mail Mailboxes for incoming mail
Run PID files, which include the ids of strolling techniques; these documents are
Frequently consulted to song or kill specific procedures
Spool documents queued or in transit, consisting of outgoing email, print jobs, and scheduled jobs
Tmp temporary storage for packages and/or humans to apply
Proc operating gadget state

5.13 Path of directories section 2: scope

The scope of a directory course describes, at an excessive stage, the purpose of an entire listing hierarchy. Some not unusual ones are:

/ system files provided with Linux (stated "root")
/usr more system documents furnished with Linux (pronounced "user")
/usr/games video games (hurray surprise!)
/usr/kerberos files concerning the Kerberos authentication system
/usr/local system files developed "domestically," either in your organization or your individual computer
/usr/X11R6 files relating the X window gadget

So, for a category like lib (libraries), your Linux gadget might have directories /lib, /usr/lib, /usr/nearby/lib, /usr/games/lib, and /usr/X11R6/lib. You may have other scopes as fits the system administrator: /my_corporation/lib, /my_department/lib, and so forth.

There isn't a clear difference among / and /usr in practice, but there is an experience that / is "lower level" and closer to the operating system. So /bin contains fundamental applications like ls and cat, /usr/bin incorporates a wide form of applications furnished together with your Linux distribution, and /usr/local/ bin incorporates applications your device administrator selected to put in. These are not hard and speedy rules however traditional instances.

5.14 Path of directories section 3: scope

The utility a part of a directory path is usually the call of a program. After the scope and category (say, /usr/local/ document), a program may additionally have its own subdirectory (say, /usr/local/document/my_program) containing files it desires.

5.15 Directories of Operating System

/lost + found
Broken documents that had been rescued through a disk recovery tool.

/boot
Documents for booting the system. That is in which the kernel lives, typically named /boot/vmlinuz.

/proc
Describes currently running processes; for super user of linux.

The files in /proc provide views into the going for walks kernel and have special homes. They constantly appear to be zero sized, examine best, and dated now:

$ ls l /proc/version
--r—r--r 1 root   root   0 Nov 21 20:45 /proc/version

However, their contents magically contain statistics about the Linux kernel:

$ cat /proc/model

Linux version 2.5.21-1.2114.nptl . . .

Ordinarily those files are utilized by applications. Cross beforehand and discover. Right here are a few examples.

/proc/uptime   device uptime, i.e., seconds elapsed for the reason that machine turned into remaining booted. Run the uptime command for a greater human readable result.

/proc/ioports   A list of your laptop's input/output hardware.

/proc/version   the working gadget model. The username command prints the identical records.

/proc/nnn   where nnn is an advantageous integer, information approximately the Linux system with process identity nnn.

/proc/self   statistics about the modern manner you're going for walks; a symbolic hyperlink to a /proc/nnn document, mechanically up to date. Try ls i/proc/ self some instances in a row: you'll see /proc/ changing in which it factors.

5.16 Protection of File

A Linux system might also have many users with login money owed. To preserve privateness and safety, every user can get entry to just a few files on the machine, not all. This access manage is embodied in two questions:

Who has permission? Every report and listing has an owner who has permission to do whatever with it. Commonly the user who created a file is its proprietor, but relationships can get more complicated.

Additionally, a predefined institution of users may additionally have perproject to get admission to a file. Companies are described by the system administrator.

Finally, a record or listing can be opened to all users with login money owed at the gadget. You will also see this set of users referred to as the world or truly other.

What kind of permission is granted? Report owners, corporations, and the arena might also every have permission to examine, write (adjust), and execute (run) unique documents. Permissions additionally enlarge to directories, which users might also read (get admission to files within the listing), write (create and delete documents inside the directory), and execute (input the listing).

Chapter 6

6.1 The Shell

With a purpose to run commands on a Linux machine, you'll need somewhere to type them. That "somewhere" is referred to as the shell, that's Linux's command line user interface: you type a command and press input, and the shell runs whatever seasone (or applications) you've requested. As an instance, to look who's logged in, you can execute this command in a shell:

```
$ who
Ben      :0 Nov 20 20:44
Jonas    pts/0  Nov 21 12:51
Younus   pts/1  Nov 22 14:15
Drake    pts/2  Nov 23 18:18
Hassan   pts/3  Nov 15:01
```

(The dollar signal is the shell activate, which means that the shell is prepared to run a command.) A single command can also invoke several packages at the identical time, and even join grams together so they have interaction. Here's a command that redirects the output of the who program to turn out to be the center of the wc program, which counts strains of textual content in a document; the result is the wide variety of strains within the output of who:

```
$ who | wc -l          number of people logged into your system
5
```

Telling you how many users are logged in. The vertical bar, called a pipe, makes the connection between who and wc. A shell is clearly a program itself, and Linux has several. We cognizance on Bash (the "Bourne again Shell"), placed in /bin/ bash, that's the Fedora Linux default.

6.2 Program vs shells

Whilst you run a command, it might invoke a Linux program (like who), or alternatively it is probably a built-in command, a feature of the shell itself. You could inform the distinction with the kind command:

$ kind who
Who is /usr/bin/who_is_user
$ type cd
Cd is a shell built in command

It is helpful to know what the shell presents versus what Linux does. The next few sections describe functions of the shell.

6.3 Features of Bash

A shell does tons extra than definitely run commands. It additionally offers effective capabilities to make this venture less difficult. Examples are wildcards for matching filenames, redirection of command output and enter to and from documents, pipes for making the output of 1 command emerge as the input of some other, aliases to run commonplace commands speedy, variables for storing values for use through the shell, and extra. We're just scratching the floor to introduce you to a fixed of useful tools. Run info bash for complete documentation.

6.4 Wildcards

Wildcards offer a shorthand for specifying sets of files with similar names. For instance, s* approach all documents whose names begin with lowercase "s". Wildcards are "elevated" through the shell into the real set of filenames they in shape. So, in case you kind:

$ ls s*

The shell first expands s* into the filenames that start with "s" for your current directory, as in case you had typed:
Ls aardvark adamantium apple ls by no means knows you used a wildcard: it sees only the final listing of filenames after the shell growth.

6.5 Brace expansion

Similar to wildcards, expressions with curly braces also expand to emerge as a couple of arguments to a command. The comma separated expression:

{a,b,cc,ddd,eeee}

Expands to:

a b cc ddd eeee

Braces work with any strings, in contrast to wildcards that are restricted to filenames. For example, Bur{A,B,CCC} ger expands to:

$ echo bur{{A,B,CCC} ger

Burager   burbbger. Burccccger

No matter what files are inside the contemporary directory.

6.6 Tilde expansion

The shell treats tildes (~) as unique characters in the event that they appear alone or at the beginning of a phrase.

~ your   own home directory
~ben   person/user ben home directory

6.7 Shell variables

You could define variables and their values via assigning them:

$ My_Variable = 5

To refer a value, certainly location a greenback register the front of the variable name:

$ echo $My_Variable = 5

To look at shell's variables, run:

$ printenv   to look at the variable of shell

The scope of the variable (i.e., which applications realize about it) is, by using default, the shell in which it's described. To make a variable and its price to be had to other programs your shell invokes (i.e., subshells), use the export command:

$ export My_Variable

Or the shorthand:

$ export My_Variable = 5

Your variable is now called a surroundings variable, because it's available to other packages to your shell's "environment." To make a particular cost available to a specific program just as soon as, prepend variable=price to the command line:

$ echo $home
/home/ben
$ home=/home/jessie echo "My home directory is $home"
My home is /home/jessie
$ echo $home
/domestic/ben   the real original value is unaffected

6.8 Search path

A totally crucial variable is path, which instructs the shell in which to discover packages. While you kind any command:
The shell has to discover this system(s) in query. It consults the price of route, which is a series of directories separated by colons:

$ echo $path
/usr/local/bin:/bin:/usr/bin:/usr/X11R6/bin:/domestic/ben/bin

And looks for the who command in every of these directories. If it unearths who (say, /usr/bin/who), it runs the command. Different smart, it reviews:

Bash: who: command not discovered

To feature directories to your shell's, seek path temporarily, modify its direction variable. For example, to append /usr/sbin for your shell's seek path:

$ path=$path:/usr/sbin
$ echo $path
/usr/local/bin:/bin:/usr/bin:/usr/X11R6/bin:/domestic/ben/bin:/usr/sbin

To make this modification everlasting, adjust the path variable on your startup report ~/.bash_profile. Then sign off and log again in.

6.9 Aliases

The integrated command alias defines a convenient shorthand for an extended command, to keep typing. For instance:

$ alias ll = 'ls -l'   shorthand for longer commands

Defines a new command ll that runs ls -l:

$ ll
Total 334
-rw-r--r-- 1 ben 3214 Nov 09 14:53 file1
-rwxr-xr-x 1 ben 42 Dec 21 21:04 file2

Define aliases for your ~/.bashrc report to be to be had whenever you log in. To peer all your aliases, kind alias. If aliases don't appear powerful enough for you (because they haven't any parameters or branching).

"Programming with Shell Scripts"

6.10 Input/output redirection

The shell can redirect preferred enter, Standard output, and standard errors to and from documents. In other phrases, any command that reads from widespread enter may have its enter come from a document alternatively with the shell's < operator:

$ mycommand < in_file   to redirect

Likewise, any command that writes to conventional output can write to a document alternatively:

```
$ mycommand > out_file    overwrite the out_file
$ mycommand >> out_file   Append to the out_file
```

A command that writes to standard errors may have its output redirected to a report as nicely:

```
$ mycommand 2> error_file          errors output redirected to a file
```

To redirect both standard output and general blunders to files:

```
$ mycommand > out_file 2> error_file    Separate the files
$ mycommand > out_file 2>&1             Single files
```

6.11 Pipes

The usage of the shell, you could redirect the standard output of 1 command to be the usual input of some other, the use of the shell's pipe (|) operator. As an example:

```
$ who | sort              redirect one output as input to other
```

Sends the output of who into the kind software, printing an alphabetically looked after listing of logged in users.

6.12 Combining commands

To invoke several instructions in sequence on a single command line, separate them with semicolons:

$ command_1 ; command_2 ; command_3

To run a sequence of instructions as above, however ,forestall execution if any of them fails, separate them with && ("and") symbols:

$ command_1 && command_2 && command_3
To run a sequence of instructions, preventing execution as quickly as one succeeds, separate them with || ("or") symbols:

$ command_1 || command2_ || command_3

6.13 Quoting

Commonly, the shell treats whitespace really as setting apart the words at the command line. If you need a phrase to contain whitespace (e.g., a filename with an area in it), surround it with single or double costs to make the shell deal with it as a unit. Single fees treat their contents literally, whilst double charges permit shell constructs be evaluated, inclusive of variables:

$ echo 'variable of home has cost of $home'
Variable of home has cost of $home
$ echo " variable of home has cost of $home'
 Variable of home has cost of /home/ben

Backquotes cause their contents to be evaluated as a command; the contents are then changed by way of the standard output of the command:

```
$ /usr/bin/whoami
Ben
$ echo My username is /usr/bin/whoami
My username is ben
```

6.14 Escaping

If an individual has unique that means to the shell but you want it used literally (e.g., * as a literal asterisk instead of a wildcard), precede the person with the backward decrease "\" individual. That is called escaping the special individual:

```
$ echo b*                As a wildcard, matching "b" filenames
Bulky big bag
$ echo b\*               As a literal asterisk
B*

$ echo "I am living in $home"     dollar signal method a variable price
I am living in /home/ben
$ echo "I am living in \$home"    A literal dollar signal
I live in $home
```

You may also break out control characters (tabs, newlines, ^D, and so on) to have them used literally at the command line, in case you precede them with ^V. This is in particular useful for tab (^I) characters, which the shell could otherwise use for filename completion.
```
$ echo "there's a tab among these can find them right  here ^V^Iand here"
```

121

There's a tab among these can find them right here   and here

6.15 Command line editing

Bash helps you to edit the command line you're operating on, using keystrokes stimulated with the aid of the textual content editors emacs and vi. To permit command line editing with emacs keys, run this command (and place it in your ~/.bash_profile to make it permanent):

$ set -o emacs   to make emacs editing permanent
For vi keys:
$ set -o vi   to make vi editing permanent

Chapter 7

7.1 Killing command line

In case you've released a command from the shell walking inside the foreground, and need to kill it straight away, type ^C. The shell acknowledges ^C as meaning, "terminate the current foreground command proper now." So, if you are displaying a completely lengthy document (say, with the cat command) and need to prevent, kind ^C:

$ cat large_file
This is a very long file containing my experiences how I have been doing Linux programming and blah blah blah as don't read it ^C
$

To kill a program running inside the historical past, you may convey it into the foreground with fg after which type ^C, or alternatively, use the kill command. In general, ^C is not a friendly manner to stop a program. If this system has its very own way to go out, use that when possible. You spot, ^C kills the program right now, not giving it any danger to clean up after itself. Killing a foreground program may go away your shell in an odd or unresponsive country, in keeping now not showing the keystrokes you type. If this occurs:

1. Press ^J to get a shell activate. This produces the same individual because the enter key (a newline) however will paintings even supposing enter does now not.
2. Type the phrase reset (although the letters don't seem even as you type) and press ^J once more to run this command. This must reset your shell.

^C works best while typed into a shell. It's going to probably have no impact if typed in a window that isn't a shell window. Additionally, some packages are written to "catch" the ^C and ignore it: an instance is the textual content editor emacs.

7.2 Terminating a Shell

To terminate a shell, both run the exit command or kind ^D.
$ exit

7.3 Tailoring Shells' behavior

To configure all your shells to work in a particular way, edit the files .bash_profile and .bashrc in your own home listing. These files execute on every occasion you log in (~/.bash_profile) or open a shell (~/.bashrc). They could set variables and aliases, run programs, print your horoscope, or something you like. Those two files are examples of shell scripts: executable files that contain shell commands.

7.4 Installing program

You will in all likelihood want to feature further program for your Linux system occasionally. The most common kinds of percent aged program for Fedora and lots of different Linux distros are:

7.4.1 *.tar.gz files, *.tar.Z documents, and *.tar.bz2 files
Compressed tar documents. They are packaged with tar and compressed with gzip (.gz), compress (.Z), or bzip2 (.bz2).

7.4.2 *.rpm files

Red Hat package supervisor (RPM) documents. Those are set up and managed with the programs rpm (manually) and up2date (robotically).

Most new program have to be installed by the superuser, so that you'll need to run the su command (or equivalent) earlier than installation. As an example:

$ su -l
Password: ******
rpm -ivh my_package.rpm
...and so forth...

To find new program, take a look at your Linux CD roms or go to excellent websites like those:
Http://freshmeat.net/ http://freshrpms.net/ http://rpmfind.internet/ http://sourceforge.internet/

7.5 Up2date

Up2date is the perfect way to preserve your Fedora device. Well, updated. As root, just run:

up2date   to keep your fedora system

And comply with the activates. This presents a graphical user interface. You can additionally run up2date in command line mode:

up2date -l   provides graphical user interface

To list all up to date RPM programs (if any) to be had in your gadget. To download the given applications, run:

up2date -d packages   to download the given packages

To put in the given RPM programs, you've got already downloaded with up2date -d, run:
up2date -i packages   given packages already installed

Up2date downloads RPM packages from purple Hat or Fedora related servers over the net, so that you may need to register your system with them the first time you run up2date.
Some Linux users choose other applications to up2date, which includes apt (http://linux.duke.edu/tasks/yum/) and apt (http://ayo.Freshrpms.net/).

7.6 Rpm

If you opt to installation RPM programs through hand, use rpm, the same package deal management program that up2date runs behind the scenes. Rpm now not best installs the software, but also makes certain your device has all stipulations. For instance, if % age super stuff requires package other stuff that you haven't hooked up, rpm will now not install super stuff. If your gadget passes the take a look at, however, rpm completely installs the software.

7.7 ls

Useful alternatives

-l lengthy long list, along with file attributes. Add the -h option ("human readable") to print document sizes in kilobytes, megabytes and gigabytes, as opposed to bytes.
-a listing of all files, along with those whose names start with a dot.
-I Prepend the inode numbers of the files.
-F beautify decorate specific filenames with meaningful symbols, indicating their types. Appends "/" to directories, "*" to executables, "@" to symbolic hyperlinks, "|" to named pipes, and "=" to sockets. Those are simply visible signs for you, no longer part of the filenames!
-s Prepend the dimensions of the report in blocks, beneficial for sorting documents by their size:

    $ ls -s | sort -n

-d If listing a listing, do not list its contents, just the listing itself.
Beneficial options
-R If listing a directory, listing its contents recursively.

7.8 Cp

-a duplicate a directory hierarchy recursively, preserving unique documents, permissions, symbolic hyperlinks, and hard link relationships. This combines the alternatives -R (recursive copy which includes unique files), -p (permissions), and -d (hyperlinks).

-p copy no longer most effective of the files permissions, however also the record's permissions, timestamps, and when you have sufficient permission to accomplish that, its proprietor and group. (usually, the copies may be owned with the aid of you, timestamped now, with permissions set with the aid of applying your unmask to the original permissions.)

-f pressure the reproduction. If a destination report exists, overwrite it unconditionally.

-i interactive mode. Ask before overwriting destination files.

7.9 ln

A hyperlink is a reference to any other document, created through the ln command. There are two styles of hyperlinks. A symbolic link refers to every other document by using its path, just like a home windows "shortcut" or a Macintosh "alias."

$ ln -s my_file soft link

In case you delete the authentic file, the now dangling link could be invalid, pointing to a nonexistent report path. A difficult hyperlink, alternatively, is absolutely a 2d name for a physical file on disk (in tech talk, it points to the identical inode). Deleting the original report does now not invalidate the hyperlink.

$ ln my_file hard link

Symbolic hyperlinks can pass disk walls, on account that they are just references to report paths; tough hyperlinks can't, since an inode on one disk has no which means on every other. Symbolic hyperlinks can also factor to directories, while tough hyperlinks cannot… Except you are the top super users and use the -d alternative.

Useful options

-i   Interactive mode. Ask earlier than overwriting destination documents.
-s Make a symbolic link. The default is a tough hyperlink.
-d allow the superuser to create a tough link to a listing.
-f force the hyperlink. If a vacation spot file exists, overwrite it unconditionally.

It's easy find out wherein a symbolic link factors with both of these commands:

$ readlink namelink

7.10 Directory Operations

Pwd Print the call of your modern listing, i.e., "wherein you are now" within the filesystem
Basename Print the very last a part of a record course
Cd trade your contemporary directory
Dirname remove / take away the very last a final part of a file direction
Mkdir Create a listing

Rmdir   Delete an empty listing

Rm -r   Delete a nonempty directory and its contents

We mentioned the listing shape of Linux in "The Filesystem" on web page thirteen. Now we'll cowl commands that create, modify, delete, and manipulate directories within that structure.

Cd

The cd (alternate directory) command sets your current working listing. And not using a listing furnished, cd defaults to your home listing.

Pwd

The cd (change listing) command units your cutting-edge running directory. And not using a directory supplied, cd defaults to your private home directory.

Basename path

The base name command prints the very last component in a record path, so for the example above:

$ basename /user/ben/my_dir
My_dir

Dirname path

The dir_name command gets rid of the very last thing from a report path:

$ dir_name /user/ben/my_dir
/user/ben

Dirname simply manipulates a string that is a directory call. It does no longer exchange your modern running directory.

Mkdir

Mkdir creates one or greater directories:

$ mkdir dir1 dir2 dir3

Useful options

-p if you deliver a directory path (not only a simple directory name), create any essential parent directories automatically: mkdir -p //one/two/three/four will create /one and /one/two in the event that they don't already exist, then /one/ two/three/four.

-m mode   Create the directory with the given permissions:

$ mkdir 0855 my_dir

By default, your shell's umask controls the permissions.

Rimdir

The rmdir (dispose of listing) command deletes one or more empty directories you name. To delete a nonempty directory and its contents, use (cautiously) rm -r listing. Use rm -ri directory to delete interactively, or rm -rf directory to annihilate with no errors messages or affirmation.

Useful alternatives

-p if you deliver a directory route (no longer only a simple directory call), delete no longer simplest the given directory, however the distinctive discern directories automatically, all of which ought to be in any other case empty. So rmdir -p /one/two/three/four will delete no longer only /one/ two/three/four, but additionally /one/two and /one if they exist.

Chapter 8

8.1 File creation and editing

To get far with Linux, you should come to be talented with one among its text editors. The two primary ones are emacs from the loose program foundation, and vim, a successor to the Unix editor vi. Teaching those editors absolutely is beyond the scope of this book. To edit a report, run both:

```
$ emacs my_file
$ vim my_file
```

If my_file doesn't exist, it is created mechanically. You may also quickly create an empty record (for later editing) the use of the touch command:

```
$ touch new_file
```

Or write statistics into a new report by using redirecting the output of a software:

$ echo whatever in any respect > new_file

If you share files with Microsoft windows structures, we are able to also cover Linux applications that edit Microsoft phrase, Excel, and PowerPoint documents.

Your Default Editor

Numerous Linux packages will run an editor while necessary, and by means of default the editor is vim. For example, your email program may invoke an editor to compose a new message, and much less invokes an editor in case you kind "v". However, what if you don't need vim to be your default editor? Set the surroundings variables visible and EDITOR on your preference, as an example:

$ EDITORIAL = emacs
$ VISIBILITY = emacs
$ export EDITORIAL VISIBILITY   totally optional

Both variables are important because distinctive applications take a look at one variable or the other. Set EDITORIAL and VISIBILITY on your ~/.bash_profile startup report in case you want your picks made permanent. Any programcan be made your default editor as long because it accepts a filename as an issue. Irrespective of the way you set those variables, all device administrators must realize as a minimum simple vim and emacs commands in case a device all at once runs an editor on an important report.

8.2 Emacs

Emacs is a very powerful enhancing surroundings with extra commands than you may possibly consider, and a whole programming language constructed in to outline your very own enhancing capabilities. To invoke the emacs tutorial, run:

$ emacs   editing environment
And sort ^h t.

Maximum emacs keystroke commands involve the manage key (like ^F) or the meta key, that's generally the ESC key or the Alt key. Emacs's own documentation notates the meta key as M- (as in M-F to intend "maintain the meta key and type F") so we are able to too.

8.3 Vim

Vim is an enhanced version of the vintage standard Unix editor vi. To run the vim tutorial, run:

$ vimtutor   enhanced UNIX editor

Vim is a mode based totally editor. It operates in two modes, insert and ordinary. Insert mode is for getting into text in the traditional manner, even as everyday mode is for walking commands like "delete a line" or copy/paste.

8.4 umask

The umask command sets or prints your default mode for creating files and directories: whether or not they are readable, writable, and/or executable by way of yourself, your group, and the world.

```
$ umask              default mode for creating files and directories
0002                 directory
$ umask -S
U=rwx, g=rwx, o=rx
```

First, a few technical communication. A umask value is a mask, i.e., a binary value that is blended (the use of the binary now not AND operation) with 0666 for files and 0777 for directories) to provide your default safety mode. As an example, 0002 not AND 0666 yields 0664 for documents, and 0002 no longer AND 0777 yields mode 0775 for directories.

8.5 soffice

Openoffice.org is a complete, included workplace program suite that can edit Microsoft phrase, Excel, and PowerPoint documents. Without a doubt run:

$ soffice   to edit Microsoft word, power point, excel files

And also, you are equipped to working with those files. The same programedits all three varieties of files. It's miles a massive program that calls for plenty of memory and disk space. Openoffice.org can also take care of drawings (sdraw command), faxes (sfax), mailing labels (slabel), and more. Http://www.openoffice.org/ has more information, or you may use the soffice assist menu.

8.6 abiword

Abiword is any other program for modifying Microsoft word documents. It's miles smaller and quicker than soffice, though not as powerful, and flawlessly suitable for many modifying duties. In case you specify documents on the command line, they have to exist: abiword would never create them for you.

8.7 gnumeric

Gnumeric is a spreadsheet programthat may edit Microsoft Excel files. It's far pretty powerful and fast, and in case you've used Excel before, gnumeric will sense acquainted. If you specify files on the command line, they need to exist: gnumeric would not create them for you.

8.8 File properties

Stat

The stat command lists crucial important attributes of files (by way of default) or filesystems (-f choice). Report information looks as if:

$ stat my_file
File: "my_file"
Size: 1264   Blocks: 8   A Fine Regular File

Access to the file : (0644/-rw-r--r--)   Uid: (600/smith) Gid:

(720/users)

Device: 30a   Inode: 99482   Links: 1

Access: Wed Jun 28.   00:16:12 2021

Modify: Wed Jul 23   23:09:41 2021

Change: Wed Jul 23   23:11:48 2021

And consists of the filename, length in bytes (1264), size in blocks (eight), document type (everyday report), permissions in octal (0644), permissions within the format of "ls -l" (-rw-r--r--), proprietor's user identity (600), owner's name (ben), owner's group identification (620), owner's institution call (users), tool type (30a), inode variety (99492), quantity of tough hyperlinks (1), and timestamps of the report's most current get right of entry to, modification, and status change. Filesystem information seems like:

$ stat -f my_file

File: "my_file"

ID: bfff357 fffffff   Name length: 255   Type EXT2

Blocks: Total: 2016068   Free: 876122   Available: 763709   Size: 4096
inodes: Total: 1026143   Free: 992372

And includes the filename (my_file), filesystem identity (bfff357 fffffff), maximum period of a filename for that filesystem (255 bytes), record-system kind (EXT2), the counts of general, free, and available blocks inside the filesystem (2016068, 876122, and 763709, respectively), block size for the filesystem (4096), and the counts of general and unfastened inodes (1026143 and 992372, respectively). The -t option provides the identical statistics however on a single line, without headings. This is reachable for processing by way of shell scripts or other packages.

Useful options

-t   Terse mode: print data on a single line.

-l   observe symbolic links and file on the document they factor to.

-f   record at the filesystem containing the file, no longer the document itself.

Wc

The wc (word count) program prints a be counted of bytes, phrases, and contours in (presumably) a text document.

$ wc my_file
22 64 424 my_file

This document has 22 lines, 64 whitespace delimited words, and 424 bytes.

Useful options

-l Print the line matter only.
-w Print the phrase count handiest.
-c Print the byte (person) matter best.
-L find the longest line in each file and print its length in bytes.

Du

The du (disk usage) command measures the disk space occupied through documents or directories. By way of default, it measures the cutting the edge directory and all its subdirectories, printing totals in blocks for every, with a grand general at the lowest.

$ du
10   ./Notes
38   ./Mail
344 ./documents/mine

By40 ./files/bobby
418 ./files
218 ./pc
2408 .

But it is able to additionally degree the dimensions of files:

$ du my_file my_file2
4 ./my_file
16 ./my_file2

Useful options

-b -k -m measure usage in bytes (-b), kilobytes (-k), or megabytes (-m)

-c Print a total in the last line. That is the default conduct when measuring a directory, however for measuring person files, provide -c in case you want a complete.

-B N   show sizes in blocks that you define, where 1 block = N bytes. (Default = 1024)

-s Print most effective the entire size.

-L follow symbolic links and degree the documents they point to.

-h -H Print "human readable" output and choose the maximum appropriate unit for every length. As an example, if two directories are of size 1 gigabyte or 25 kilobytes, respectively, du -h prints 1G and 25K. The -h option uses powers of 1024 while -H uses powers of one thousand.

Chmod [options] permission files

The chmod (exchange mode) command units set access permissions for files and directories. Not each file ought to be to be had to anyone (this isn't windows 95, you realize), and chmod is the device for ensuring this. Common permissions are read, write, and execute, and they may be confined to the record proprietor, the report's institution proprietor, and/or other users. The permissions argument can take 3 distinctive forms:

- --reference=files, to set the same permissions as any other given file
- One or more strings specifying absolute or relative permissions (i.e., relative to the file's existing permissions) to be carried out, separated via commas.
- An octal number, up to 4 digits long, that specifies the document's absolute permissions in bits. The leftmost digit is special (defined later) and the second one, 0.33, and fourth represent the file's owner, the report's institution, and all users. See parent 3 for an instance, showing the that means of mode 0640.

Figure 8.1

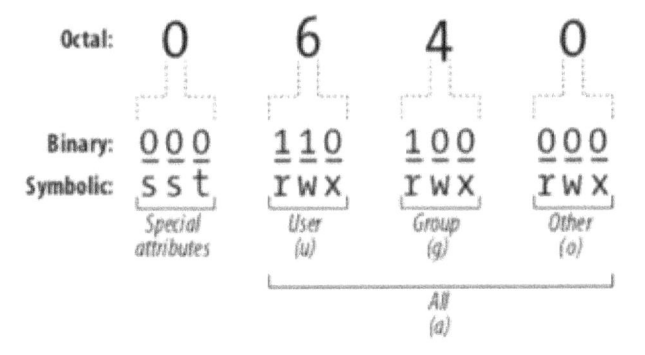

	Octal	Binary	Symbolic	
	0	0 0 0	s s t	Special attributes
	6	1 1 0	r w x	User (u)
	4	1 0 0	r w x	Group (g)
	0	0 0 0	r w x	Other (o)

All (a)

Within the third shape, each string includes three components: an optionally available scope, a command, and permissions.

Scope (optionally available)

U for user, g for organization, o for other users now not within the institution, for all users. The default is a.

Command

+ to feature permissions, -to take away permissions, = to set absolute permissions, ignoring existing ones

Permissions

R for examine, w for write/modify, x for execute (for directories, this is permission to cd into the listing), X for conditional execute (explained later), u to replicate the user permissions, g to duplicate the institution permissions, o to duplicate the "different users" permissions, s for setuid or setgid, and t for the sticky bit.

For instance, ug+rw could add study and write permission for the user and the organization, a-x (or just -x) would get rid of execute permission for everyone, and u=r would first remove all present permissions and then make the file readable best by means of its owner. You could integrate those strings by means of separating them with commas, along with ug+rw, a-x.

Setuid and setgid practice to executable files (packages and scripts). Think we've got an executable record F owned through user "ben" and the organization "buddies". If record F has setuid (set person id) enabled, then anyone who runs F will "turn out to be" user ben, with all her rights and privileges, all through the program. Likewise, if F has setgid (set institution identification) enabled, anybody who executes F turns into a member of the pals institution at some stage in this system. As you may think, setuid and setgid can affect system protection, so don't use them except you truly understand what you're doing. One out of place chmod +s can go away your whole machine at risk of assault.

Conditionals execute permission (X) method the same as x, except that it succeeds only if the document is already executable, or if the record is a listing. In any other case it has no effect.

Useful alternatives

-R   Recursively alternate the ownership within a directory hierarchy.

8.9 Find Location

Find   discover and locate files in a listing hierarchy
Slocate   Create an index of documents, and search the index for string
Which   locate executables in your search direction (command)
Type   locate executables to your seek route (bash h built in)
Whereis   discover and locate executables, documentation, and source file

Linux systems can contain tens or hundreds of hundreds of files without problems. How will you discover a particular record when you want to? Step one is to organize your files logically into directories in a few thoughtful way, however there are numerous different methods to discover files, depending on what you are searching out. For locating any report, find is a brute force program that slogs file by way of record thru a listing hierarchy to find a target. Slocate is much quicker, looking through a prebuilt index that you generate as needed. (Fedora generates the index nightly via default.) For locating applications, the which and sort instructions take a look at all directories to your shell seek course. Type is constructed into the bash shell (and consequently to be had simplest when strolling bash), even as which is an application (commonly /usr/bin/which); type is faster and can detect shell aliases. In evaluation, where is examines an acknowledged set of directories, as opposed to your seek course.

8.10 Indexing options

-u.   Create index from the foundation directory downward.
-l (0|1)   flip safety off (zero) or on (1). The default is 1.
-U directory   Create index from directory towards downward.
-o outfile   Write the index to file of outfile.

-e directories   Exclude one or greater directories from the index. Separate their paths by   means of commas.

Search Options

Index regexp
Create index from directory downward.

-r regexp   look for files matching the given normal expression.
-d indexes   indicate which index to use (in our instance, /tmp/my_index).
-i   Case insensitive search.

Which file

The which command locates an executable files in your shell's seek path. If you've been invoking a program with the aid of typing its name:

$ who   locates an executable file in shell search path

The which command tells you in which this command is positioned:

```
$ which who      tell where the command is positioned
/usr/bin/who     location
```

You may even locate the which program itself:

```
$ which which          can search for where which program is
positioned
/usr/bin/which         location
```

If several applications in your search route have the identical name (say, /usr/bin/who and /usr/local/bin/who), which reports best the first.

8.11 File Text Manipulation

One among Linux's greatest strengths is text manipulation: massaging a text file (or preferred input) right into a desired form via making use of variations. Any application that reads known input and writes preferred output falls into this class, but here we'll present some of the maximum common and powerful.

Grep

The grep command is one of the most continually beneficial and effective inside the Linux arsenal. Its premise is straightforward: given one or greater documents, print all strains in the ones files that healthy a specific ordinary expression sample. For example, if a file contains those traces:
Youth radicalization has been an issue since forever and it has global effects.
Seeing is believing but feeling is the truth.
Books give me another world.

And we search for all lines containing "pancake", we get:

$ grep effects my_file
Youth radicalization has been an issue since forever and it has global effects.

Grep can use exceptional forms of everyday expressions, which it calls simple and extended. They're equally powerful, simply exceptional, and you can choose one over the alternative based in your enjoy with different grep implementations.

8.12 File Comparison

There are three methods to compare Linux files:

- Line through line (diff, diff3, sdiff, comm), great proper to textual text files
- by way of evaluating checksums (md5sum, sum, cksum)
- Byte by way of byte (cmp), often used for binary files

Those applications are all textual content based. For a graphical document comparison device, try xxdiff at http://xxdiff.sourceforge.internet.

Diff [options] file1, file2

The diff command compares two files line by line, or directories. While comparing textual content files, diff can produce special reviews of their differences. For binary documents, diff simply reports whether they fluctuate or now not. For all files, if there are not any differences, diff produces no output.

The traditional output format looks as if this:

Indication of line numbers and the type of change
< Corresponding segment of file1, if any
> Corresponding section of file2, if any
For instance, if we begin with a file filex:

Hello, this is a really nice file.
Youth radicalization has been an issue since forever and it has global effects.
Seeing is believing but feeling is the truth.
Books give me another world.

Assume we delete the primary line, exchange "global" to "local" on the second one line, and upload a final line, creating a report filey:

Youth radicalization has been an issue since forever and it has local effects.
Seeing is believing but feeling is the truth.
Books give me another world.
Have a good day!

Then diff filex filey produces this output:
1,2c1   filex lines 1-2 became filey line 1
< hello, this is a really nice file.   Lines 1-2 of filex
< Youth radicalization has been an issue since forever and it has global effects.
-----   diffractal separator
> Youth radicalization has been an issue since forever and it has local effects.   Line 1 of filey
>   Have   a   good   day!

Appended line

The main symbols < and > are arrows indicating filex and filey, respectively. This output format is the default: many others are available, a number of which may be fed without delay to different equipment.

Diff can also compare the directories: $ diff dir1 dir2

Which compares any same named documents in those directories and lists all files that appear in a single listing but now not the other. If you need to examine whole listing hierarchies, recursively, use the -r option:
$ diff -r dir1 dir2

Chapter 9

9.1 Disks and file system

Df   show to be had area on established filesystems
Umount Unmount a disk partition (make it inaccessible)
Mount   Make a disk partition on hand
Sync   Flush all disk caches to disk
Fsck   test a disk partition for errors

Linux systems will have multiple disks or disk partitions. In casual communique, these are variously referred to as disks, partitions, filesystems, volumes, even directories. We'll try to be greater accurate. A disk is a hardware device, which can be divided into partitions that act as unbiased storage devices. Walls are represented on Linux structures as special files in (typically) the /dev listing. As an example, /dev/hda7 can be a partition on your grasp IDE disk. A few common devices in /dev are:

hda   First IDE bus, is a master device; partitions are hda1, hda2
hdb   First IDE bus, is a slave device; walls of partitions are hdb1, hdb2
hdc   second IDE bus, master tool; walls of partition are hdc1, hdc2
hdd   second IDE bus, slave tool device; partitions are hdd1, hdd2
sda   First SCSI device; walls are sda1, sda2
sdb   2nd SCSI tool; partitions are sdb1, sdb2, Likewise for sdc, sdd
ht0   First IDE tape pressure (then ht1, ht2) with auto rewind
nht0   First IDE tape drive (then nht1, nht2,) Without auto rewind
st0 First SCSI tape force (then st1, st2,)
Scd0   First SCSI CD-ROM force (then scd1, scd2)

156

Fd0   First floppy power (then fd1, fd2), commonly mounted on /mnt/floppy

Earlier than a partition can preserve files, it is "formatted" by writing a filesystem on it. A filesystem defines how files are represented; examples are ext3 (Linux journaling filesystem, the Fedora default) and vfat (Microsoft windows filesystem). Formatting is normally done for you when putting in Linux. Once a filesystem is created, you can make it to be had for use with the aid of mounting it on an empty listing. For instance, in case you mount a home windows filesystem on a directory /mnt/win, it turns into part of your gadget's listing tree, and you could create and edit files like /mnt/win/my_file. Filesystems can also be unmounted to lead them to inaccessible, say, for maintenance. Mounting of difficult drives is commonly executed automatically at boot time.

Df [options] [disk devices| files |directories]

The df (disk unfastened) software suggests you the size, used area, and free space on a given disk partition. In case you supply a document or directory, df describes the disk device on which that files or directory is living. Without an arguments, df reviews on all mounted filesystems.

Mount

The mount command makes a hardware storage device reachable. Maximum typically it handles disk devices (say, /dev/hda1), making them accessible via a current listing (say, /mnt/my_dir):

```
# mkdir /mnt/my_dir
# mount /dev/hda1 /mnt/my_dir
# df /mnt/my_dir
```

Filesystem 1K-blocks Used available Use% installed on /dev/hda1 1011928 285744 674780 30% /mnt/my_dir mount has lots of alternatives and makes use of; we will speak only the most basic.

In most common instances, mount reads the report /and many others/fstab (filesystem table) to learn how to mount a favored disk. For instance, if you kind mount /usr, the mount command seems up the "/usr" line in /etc./fstab, which might look like this:

/dev/hda8 /usr ext3 defaults 1 2   mount reads the file to learn how to mount a desired disk

Here mount learns, among different matters, that disk tool /dev/hda8 have to be hooked up on /usr as a Linux ext3-formatted filesystem. Mount is run generally by means of the superuser, but common gadgets like floppy and CD-ROM drives regularly may be set up and unmounted by means of any person.

$ mount /mnt/cdrom   the cdrom can be mounted and unmounted
$ mount /mnt/floppy   the floppy disk can be mounted and unmounted

Umount [options] [device] [directory]

Umount is the other of mount: it makes a disk partition unavailable a position. As an instance, if you've established a CD-ROM disc, you might not eject it until it's umounted:

$ umount /mnt/cdrom   makes partition unavailable

Usually unmount detachable media before ejecting it or you danger harm to its filesystem. To unmount all set up devices:
umount -a

Sync

The sync command flushes all disk caches to disk. Typically, the kernel may additionally buffer reads, writes, inode adjustments, and different disk- associated activity in memory. Sync writes the adjustments to disk. Commonly, you don't need to run this command, however if (say) you're about to do something unstable that would crash your gadget, walking sync right now in advance can't harm.

9.2 Partitioning and Formatting Disks

Disk associated operations like partitioning and formatting can be complicated on Linux structures. Here are guidelines to the pro- grams you may need (start with their manpages).

Parted, fdisk or sfdisk   Partition a difficult force. Any of those programs will do they without a doubt have distinct person interfaces.
Floppy   formats a floppy disk.
Mkfs   layout a difficult disk, i.e., create a new filesystem.

9.3 Backups and remote storage

mt   control a tape power
rsync   mirror a hard and fast of files onto every other tool or host
dump   Write a disk partition to tape
cdrecord   Burn a CD-R
Restore   it restores the effects of a dump
tar   read and write tape data

There are various manner to returned up your precious Linux files:

- Burn them onto a CD-R
- Copy them to a tape drive
- Mirror them onto the remote device

Your tape backup tool is usually /dev/ht0 for an IDE force, or /dev/st0 for a SCSI drive (or for an IDE pressure using idscsi emulation). It's not unusual to make a hyperlink referred to as /dev/tape to the proper device:

$ ln -s /dev/ht0 /dev/tape   to make link appropriate device

We aren't offering every Linux command for backups. Some users decide upon cpio to tar, and for low level disk copies, dd is priceless. See the manpages for those packages if you are inquisitive about them.

9.4 File Printing

lpr	it prints the file
lpq	it View the print queue
lprm	dispose of a print task from the queue

Linux has two popular printing systems, referred to as CUPS and lprng; Fedora comes with CUPS. Each structures use commands with the identical names: lpr, lpq, and lprm. However, those instructions have distinct options depending on whether or not you're the usage of CUPS or lprng. To be usually helpful, we are able to gift not unusual alternatives that work with both structures. To install a printer to be used with Fedora, run the command:

redhat-config-printer   to install a printer to be use with fedora

And comply with the guidelines and directions.

9.5 Spelling Operations

look   appearance up the spelling of a phrase fast
spell   Batch spelling checker
aspell   Interactive spelling checker

Linux has numerous spellcheckers constructed in. If you're accustomed to graphical spellcheckers, you may locate Linux's fairly primitive, but they may be used in pipelines, that's pretty effective.

Look

The look command prints (on general output) phrases that start with a given string prefix. The words are placed in a dictionary document (default /usr/share/dict/phrases). As an example, appearance big prints:

Large
Larger
Largest

If you deliver your very own dictionary report any textual content record with alphabetically taken care of strains look will print all lines starting with the given prefix.

Spell

The spell command prints all words inside the given files which can be misspelled, in line with its dictionary. It's similar to:

$ cat documents | aspell -l | sort -u   gives misspelled words in a file

If no files are provided, spell reads from standard input

9.6 Viewing processes

Ps   lists the process
Uptime   inspects and view the system load
W   listing of the active methods for all users
Top   provides the top class monitoring of resource intensive processes interactively
Xload   monitor device load graphically in an X window
Free   show loose free memory

A manner is a unit of work on a Linux system. Each application you run represents one or more processes, and Linux commands for viewing and manipulating them. Each manner is recognized by way of a numeric system id, or PID. Strategies are not the same as other methods are part of the running gadget, whereas jobs are regarded most effective to the shell wherein they are walking. A strolling application accommodates one or greater methods; a job consists of 1 or greater packages finished as a shell command.

9.7 Controlling methods

Kill   Terminates a system process (or ship it a sign)
Nice   Invoke a software program at a specific precedence
Renice   change a technique's precedence as it runs

As soon as approaches are started, they can be stopped, restarted, killed, and reprioritized. We discussed a number of those operations as handled via the shell in "activity control" Now we cover killing and reprioritizing.

Kill [options] [process_ids]

The kill command sends a sign to a system. This will terminate a technique (the default), interrupt it, suspend it, crash it, and so forth. You need to personal the system, or be the superuser, to have an effect on it.

$ kill 13243   sends signal to process to get terminate or crash

If this does not work some programs seize this signal without terminating upload the -KILL alternative:

$ kill -KILL 13243   use this command if prior one does not work

That's definitely assured to work. But this isn't a smooth go out for the program, which might also depart assets allotted (or different inconsistencies) upon its death. In case you don't understand the PID of a process, attempt the pidof command:

$ /sbin/pidof emacs   PID of process

Or run ps and examine the output.

Similarly, to this system /bin/kill within the filesystem, most shells have integrated kill instructions, but their syntax and conduct vary. But they all help this utilization:
$ kill -N PID   N is the number of signals

Wherein N is a signal number, and call is a sign name without its main "SIG" (e.g., use -HUP to send the SIGHUP signal). To look an entire listing of indicators transmitted by way of kill, run kill -l, even though its output differs relying on which kill you are running.

Nice [-priority] command_line

Whilst invoking a device-in depth application, you would possibly want to be fine to the alternative techniques (and customers) with the aid of lowering its precedence. That's what the exceptional command is for. Right, here's an example of setting a massive job to run at priority 7:

$ first-class -7 type Very_Large_File > outfile

If you don't specify a priority, 10 is used. To find out the default priority (i.e., what you had get in case you didn't run high-quality), kind nice without an arguments:

$ nice   to find out the default priority
0

In case you're the superuser, you can also increase the priority (lower the wide variety):

$ nice - -10   super user can increase the priority

(yes, that's "dash negative 10".) To see the great ranges of your jobs, use ps and study the "NI" column:

$ ps -o pid, consumer, arg, nice   at nice levels of your jobs

Renice

Even as the satisfactory command can invoke an application at a given precedence, renice modifications the priority of an already running technique. Here we growth the fine stage (decrease the concern) of system 28734 by 5:

```
$ renice +10 -p 28734
```

Ordinary user can lower priorities (boom the variety), and the superuser can enhance priorities (lower the wide variety). The legitimate range is −20 to +20, however keep away from exceedingly poor numbers or you might intervene with essential system approaches.

9.8 Customers and their environment

Log name just Print your login name
whoami it simply Prints your current, effective username
id Print the user identification and institution membership of a consumer
who it shows listing logged in users, long output!
users it shows listing logged in users, quick short output
finger this print facts approximately users determine whilst someone remaining logged in
printenv it simply Print your environment

Who are you? Handiest the system is aware of for certain. This grasp of packages tells you all approximately users: their names, login times, and houses in their environment.

Logname

The logname command prints your login name. It might appear Trivial, but it's useful in shell scripts.

$ logname ben

Whoami

The whoami command prints the name of the contemporary, effective user. This may differ out of your login name (the output of logname) if you've used the su command. This case distinguishes whoami from logname:

```
$ logname ben
$ whoami ben
$ su
Password: ******
# logname
Ben
# whoami
Root
```

Identification

Every person has a completely unique, numeric person id, and a default organization with a unique, numeric group id. The id command prints these values together with their associated person and group names:

```
$ id            prints id
Uid=500(ben)                              gid=500(ben)
companies=500(ben),6(disk),490(src),501(cdwrite)
```

Who

The who command lists all logged in customers, one person shell per line:

```
  $ who

Ben      :0.        Sep 8 17:02
Younus   pts/1      Sep 8 17:11
Bella    pts/2      Sep 9 20:52
Edward   pts/4      Sep 4 05:12
```

Commonly, who gets its records from the report /var/run/utmp. The filename argument can specify a distinctive information document, consisting of /var/log/wtmp for past logins or /var/log/btmp for failed logins.

User [filename]

The customers command prints a short list of users who have login classes. If a consumer is running a couple of shells, she appears a couple of times.

$ users
Edward bella ben ben ben

Like the who command, customers reads /var/log/utmp with the aid of default but can study from any other provided file as an alternative.

Last

The final command presentations a history of logins, in reverse chronological order.

$ last   displays history of logins

Edward pts/3 localhost Mon Sep 10 21:01 21:08 (00:07) ben pts/6 :0 Mon Sep 8 20:24 20:56 (00:32) Edward pts/4 my_host sun Sep 7 22:13 nonetheless logged in you can provide usernames or tty names to restrict the output.

Chapter 10

10.1 Network connections

Ssh Securely log right into a far remote host or run commands on it.
Telnet Log right into a far on remote host a bit insecure.
Scp Securely copy files to/from a far remote host in batch form.
Sftp Securely copy files to/from a remote host (interactive)
Ftp copies documents to/from a remote host interactive and insecure.

With Linux, it's easy to establish community connections from one gadget to some other for faraway logins and report transfers. Simply make sure you do it securely.

Ssh

The ssh (relaxed Shell) program securely logs you into a remote device wherein you have already got an account:

$ ssh   example.com

Instead, it can invoke a program on that remote gadget without logging you in:

$ ssh example.com who

Ssh encrypts all facts that travels throughout its connection, which include your username and password (that you'll need to access the remote device). The SSH protocol also supports different approaches to authenticate, together with public keys and host ids. See man sshd for details.

Useful options

-l username Specify your faraway username; otherwise, ssh assumes your neighborhood username. You may additionally use the syntax user_name@host:

$ ssh ben@server.instance.com

-p port   Use a port number other than the default port which is 22.
-t   Allocate a tty on the remote device; beneficial while seeking to run a far flung
Command with an interactive user interface, inclusive of a textual text editor.
-v.   Produce verbose output, useful for debugging.

Telnet

The telnet program logs you into a remote device in which you have already got an account.
$ telnet remote.someexample.com

Keep away from telnet for remote logins: maximum implementations are insecure and send your password over the network in undeniable text for all of us to thieve. Use ssh as a substitute, which protects your password and facts through encryption. There are two exceptions:

- In a Kerberos environment, using greater ("kerberized") Telnet software on each the consumer and server facet). Fedora telnet can work with Kerberos. See http://internet.mit.edu/ kerberos/ for extra statistics.

- Connecting to a remote port while you aren't sending any touchy data in any respect. As an example, to test for the presence of a web server (port eighty) on a remote machine:

```
$ telnet remote.someexample.com 80
Trying 192.168.55.21
Connected to remote.someexample.com (192.168.55.21).
ESC character is '^]'.
Xxx type some words and press the enter button
<HTML><HEAD>    # it's a web browser
<Title> 400 that's a bad request</title>
</HEAD><BODY>
<H1>bad Request</H1>
Your browser has sent a request that
This server could not recognize.<P> </body></HTML>
Connection has been closed by using foreign host.
```

To discourage you further from the usage of telnet, we aren't even going to explain its alternatives.

Scp

The scp (at ease reproduction) command copies files and directories from one computer to every other in batch. (For an interactive consumer inter- face, see sftp.) It encrypts all verbal exchange between the two machines.

```
$ scp my_file remote.someexample.com:newfile
$ scp -r my_dir remote.someexample.com
$ scp remote.someexample.com:myfile .
$ scp -r remote.someexample.com:mydir .
```

To specify an alternate username at the faraway device, use the user_name@host syntax:

$ scp my_file ben@remote.someexample.com:

Useful alternatives

-p   duplicate all file attributes (permissions, timestamps) whilst copying.
-v   Produce verbose output, beneficial for debugging.

-r   Recursively copy a listing and its contents.

Sftp

The sftp software copies files interactively among two computer systems. (as opposed to scp, which copies documents in batch.) The person interface is much like that of ftp.

$ sftp remote.someexample.com
Password: ******
Sftp> cd My_Files
Sftp > ls
README
File_1
File_2
File_3
Sftp > get file_2
Fetching /home/ben/My_Files/file_2 to file_2
Sftp > end

If your username at the remote system is different from your local one, use the user_name@host argument:
$ sftp ben@remotef.someexample.com

Ftp

The ftp (report switch Protocol) program copies documents between computer systems, however now not in a secure manner: your username and bypass the word travel over the community as plain textual content. Use sftp alternatively whenever feasible. The identical commands we indexed for sftp also paintings for ftp. (but, the 2 applications support different, differing instructions, too.)

Email

Evolution	GUI email client
Mail	minimum text mail client
Mutt	textual content mail purchaser

Fedora consists of some of mail readers. We'll take a look at three with exceptional purposes and strengths. Different Linux mailers include pine, the RMAIL and vm packages built into emacs, and Mozilla's Mail & news. To peer the progress of e mail messages you ship and receive, view the logfile /var/log/mail_log. As root, you can use the mail command to view any outgoing mail messages nevertheless queued on your system, waiting to be sent.

10.2 Evolution

Ximian Evolution is a graphical email application that looks loads like Microsoft Outlook. Depending on how your device is set up, you can invoke Evolution from the principal menu as net : Evolution email, or via running the command evolution from the shell.

To installation a mail account:

1. Select tool → Settings.
2. Inside the Evolution Settings window, if you do now not already have an electronic mail account indexed, pick add. Otherwise, choose the account and select Edit.
3. Within the Evolution Account Editor window, the identity tab, fill to your complete call and electronic mail deal with.
4. Pick out the Receiving Mail tab and the Server kind (IMAP, POP, local shipping, and so forth) and fill within the fields relevant to your mail server. For POP or IMAP servers, fill within the mail server host and username supplied by your ISP; for local transport, fill in the course in your neighborhood mailbox.
5. Choose the Sending Mail tab and pick out the sort of your outgoing mail server: SMTP if the server is remote (you'll be brought about for the hostname) or send mail if the server is the local system.
6. The relaxation of the tabs and options are at your discretion. Select good enough to exit the Evolution Account Editor. You ought to be prepared for primary mail operations.

Inbox   to View your mail
New   use to Compose a new mail message
Send/receive   take a look at for new mail
Reply   to reply to a message, best to the sender
Reply to All   respond to a message, to all addresses in the To and CC lines
Forward   ahead to forward a message to a third party.

10.3 Mutt [options]

Mutt is a textual text mailer that runs in an ordinary terminal (or terminal window), so it may be used both locally (e.g., in an X terminal window) or remotely over an SSH connection. It's far very powerful, with many commands and options. To invoke it, kind:

$ mutt   text mailer

While the primary screen seems, any messages for your mailbox are listed in brief, one in step with line.

10.4 Mail

The mail software (equivalently, Mail) is a short, easy email consumer. The majority need an extra effective program for everyday use, but for short messages from the command line or in scripts, mail is certainly accessible.

To send a short message:

$ mail ben@someexample.com
Subject: my subject
I typing a text message.
To end the text message, I will type a period itself on the end of it.
.
Cc: Awais@someexample.com
$

To ship a short message the usage of a single command:

$ echo "have a good day" | mail -s "subject" ben@someexample.com

To mail a record the use of a single command, use both of these:

$ mail -s "my subject" ben@someexample.com < file_name
$ cat file_name | mail -s "my subject" ben@someexample.com

Observe how without difficulty you may ship the output of a pipeline as an email message.

Useful options

-s subject Set the subject line for the outgoing message.

-c address CC the message to the given addresses, for the comma separated listing.

-b address BCC the message to the given addresses, a comma separated list.

-v Verbose mode: print the messages for the mail delivery.

13.1 Conclusion

13.1.1 Final words

Although we've included many commands and competencies of Linux, we have simply scratched the surface. Fedora and different distributions come with hundreds of different applications. We encourage you to hold analyzing, exploring, and learning the talents of your Linux structures. Appropriate good fortune!

Lightning Source UK Ltd.
Milton Keynes UK
UKHW022106110621
385375UK00002B/369

9 781802 269918